FREE DVD  FREE DVD

From Stress to Success DVD from Trivium Test Prep

Dear Customer,

Thank you for purchasing from Trivium Test Prep! Whether you're looking to join the military, get into college, or advance your career, we're honored to be a part of your journey.

To show our appreciation (and to help you relieve a little of that test-prep stress), we're offering a **FREE *From Stress to Success* DVD** by Trivium Test Prep. Our DVD includes thirty-five test preparation strategies that will help keep you calm and collected before and during your big exam. All we ask is that you email us your feedback and describe your experience with our product. Amazing, awful, or just so-so: we want to hear what you have to say!

To receive your **FREE *From Stress to Success* DVD**, please email us at 5star@triviumtestprep. com. Include "Free 5 Star" in the subject line and the following information in your email:

1. The title of the product you purchased.

2. Your rating from 1 – 5 (with 5 being the best).

3. Your feedback about the product, including how our materials helped you meet your goals and ways in which we can improve our products.

4. Your full name and shipping address so we can send your **FREE *From Stress to Success* DVD**.

If you have any questions or concerns please feel free to contact me directly.

Thank you, and good luck with your studies!

Alyssa Wagoner
Quality Control
alyssa.wagoner@triviumtestprep.com

D1571366

ACCUPLACER
Practice Tests
350 Test Prep Questions for the Accuplacer Exam

Copyright © 2016 by Trivium Test Prep

ALL RIGHTS RESERVED. By purchase of this book, you have been licensed one copy for personal use only. No part of this work may be reproduced, redistributed, or used in any form or by any means without prior written permission of the publisher and copyright owner.

Trivium Test Prep is not affiliated with or endorsed by any testing organization and does not own or claim ownership of any trademarks, specifically for the ACCUPLACER exam. All test names (and their acronyms) are trademarks of their respective owners. This study guide is for general information and does not claim endorsement by any third party.

Printed in the United States of America.

TABLE OF CONTENTS

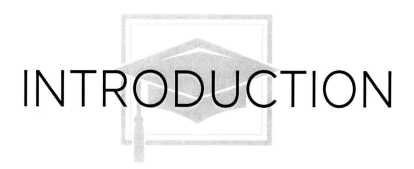

INTRODUCTION

Congratulations on choosing to take the ACCUPLACER! By purchasing this book, you've taken the first step toward preparing for your college and career goals.

This guide will provide you with a detailed overview of the ACCUPLACER so you know exactly what to expect on test day. We'll take you through all the concepts covered on the test and give you the opportunity to test your knowledge with practice questions. Even if it's been a while since you last took a major test, don't worry; we'll make sure you're more than ready!

WHAT IS THE ACCUPLACER?

The ACCUPLACER assesses students' abilities in reading, writing and mathematics, helping them prepare for college-level courses. These tests will help you and your academic advisors choose which classes are right for you as you get ready for academic work at the university level.

WHAT'S ON THE ACCUPLACER?

The ACCUPLACER assesses basic reading comprehension, writing, and arithmetic skills. Depending on a students' abilities on these questions, it will present more difficult questions: college-level mathematics including algebra, coordinate geometry, and trigonometry, and ESL-level comprehension and language skills questions. A student may take any or all of the tests outlined below:

ACCUPLACER outline

SECTION	CONCEPTS	NUMBER OF QUESTIONS
Arithmetic	Operations with whole numbers, fractions, decimals, percentages, and applications.	17 questions
College-level math	Algebraic operations and applications; word problems; equations and inequalities; coordinate geometry; trigonometry and functions	20 questions
Elementary algebra	Operations with integers, rational numbers, algebraic expressions; solving equations, inequalities, and word problems	12 questions
Reading comprehension	Main ideas, supporting ideas, drawing inferences, identifying details	20 questions

Sentence skills	Sentence structure and clarity	20 questions
WritePlacer (essay)	Effective, organized writing with supported and well-developed ideas, strong sentence structure, and few mechanical errors	1 essay (300 – 600 words)
ESL—language use	Grammar and usage	20 questions
ESL—listening	Comprehension of spoken English	20 questions
ESL—reading skills	Comprehension of English-language reading (short and mid-length passages)	20 questions
ESL—science meaning	Comprehension of English-language sentences	20 questions

HOW IS THE ACCUPLACER SCORED?

The ACCUPLACER is a diagnostic test; as such, it is not scored and there is no way to pass or fail it. This computer-based test adapts to the student's skill level: a student's response to a question determines the difficulty level of the next one.

HOW IS THE ACCUPLACER ADMINISTERED?

The ACCUPLACER is a multiple-choice test administered by computer. The ESL – Listening section may be administered as a conversation. The exam is not timed. Students must directly contact their college counseling office in order to arrange to take the ACCUPLACER. Your institution's test center will provide information about accommodation for disabilities, required identification or materials, and any options for taking the test remotely.

HOW DOES THIS BOOK WORK?

Because we have eliminated "filler" or "fluff," you'll be able to work through the guide at a significantly faster pace than you would with other test prep books. By allowing you to focus only on those concepts that will increase your score, we'll make your study time shorter and more effective.

Now that you have a firm understanding of the exam and what is included our book, don't forget that learning how to study, as well as how to successfully pass an exam, is just as important as the content. Trivium Test Prep would like to remind you as you begin your studies that we are offering a **FREE** *From Stress to Success* **DVD**. Our DVD includes thirty-five test preparation strategies that will help keep you calm and collected before and during your big exam. All we ask is that you email us your feedback and describe your experience with our product. Amazing, awful, or just so-so: we want to hear what you have to say!

To receive your **FREE *From Stress to Success* DVD**, please email us at 5star@triviumtestprep.com. Include

"Free 5 Star" in the subject line and the following information in your email:

1. The title of the product you purchased.
2. Your rating from 1 – 5 (with 5 being the best).
3. Your feedback about the product, including how our materials helped you meet your goals and ways in which we can improve our products.
4. Your full name and shipping address so we can send your **FREE *From Stress to Success* DVD**.

We hope you find the rest of this study guide helpful.

TEST YOUR
KNOWLEDGE

PRACTICE TEST ONE

ARITHMETIC

1. $5 - 3 \times 2 + 7 =$

  A) 6

  B) 11

  C) 18

  D) 22

2. $3.819 + 14.68 + 0.0006 =$

  A) 5.2846

  B) 18.4996

  C) 18.505

  D) 52.96

3. Which of the following is closest to $15{,}886 \times 210$?

  A) 33,000

  B) 330,000

  C) 3,300,000

  D) 33,000,000

4. A landscaping company charges 5 cents per square foot for fertilizer. How much would they charge to fertilize a 30 foot by 50 foot lawn?

  A) $7.50

  B) $15.00

  C) $75.00

  D) $150.00

5. $\frac{15}{25} =$

  A) 0.06

  B) 0.15

  C) 0.375

  D) 0.6

6. 15 is 8 percent of what number?

  A) 1.2

  B) 53.3

  C) 120

  D) 187.5

7. A woman's dinner bill comes to $48.30. If she adds a 20% tip, what will she pay in total?

  A) $9.66

  B) $38.64

  C) $57.96

  D) $68.30

8. In a neighborhood, $\frac{2}{5}$ of the houses are painted yellow. If there are 24 houses that are not painted yellow, how many yellow houses are in the neighborhood?

  A) 16

  B) 9.6

  C) 24

  D) 40

9. $54.48 \div 0.6 =$

   A) 0.908

   B) 9.08

   C) 90.8

   D) 908

10. $\frac{8}{15} \div \frac{1}{6} =$

    A) $\frac{4}{45}$

    B) $\frac{15}{48}$

    C) $\frac{16}{5}$

    D) $\frac{46}{15}$

11. Five numbers have an average of 16. If the first four numbers have a sum of 68, what is the fifth number?

    A) 12

    B) 16

    C) 52

    D) 80

12. The measures of two angles of a triangle are 25° and 110°. What is the measure of the third angle?

    A) 40°

    B) 45°

    C) 50°

    D) 55°

13. What percent of 14 is 35?

    A) 4.9

    B) 2.5

    C) 40

    D) 250

14. Megan has $\frac{13}{16}$ of a cake left. If her dad eats $\frac{1}{3}$ of the remaining cake, what proportion of the cake is left?

    A) $\frac{1}{4}$

    B) $\frac{13}{24}$

    C) $\frac{1}{2}$

    D) $\frac{3}{4}$

15. Which of the following is the greatest?

    A) 0.203

    B) 0.32

    C) 0.023

    D) 0.032

16. A restaurant employs servers, hosts, and managers in a ratio of 9:2:1. If there are 36 total employees, how many hosts work at the restaurant?

    A) 3

    B) 4

    C) 6

    D) 8

17. $1\frac{3}{4} + 2\frac{3}{8} =$

    A) $3\frac{3}{4}$

    B) $3\frac{7}{8}$

    C) 4

    D) $4\frac{1}{8}$

18. $4 - \frac{1}{2^2} + 24 \div (8 + 12)$

    Simplify the expression. Which of the following is correct?

    A) 1.39

    B) 2.74

    C) 4.95

    D) 15.28

19. $(6.4)(2.8) \div 0.4$

    Simplify the expression. Which of the following is correct?

    A) 16.62

    B) 17.92

    C) 41.55

    D) 44.80

ELEMENTARY ALGEBRA

1. What is the value of the expression $\frac{x^2 - 2y}{y}$ when $x = 20$ and $y = \frac{x}{2}$?

   A) 0

   B) 19

   C) 36

   D) 38

2. $3x^3 + 4x - (2x + 5y) + y =$

   A) $11x - 4y$

   B) $29x - 4y$

   C) $3x^3 + 2x - 4y$

   D) $3x^3 + 2x + y$

3. If $10y - 8 - 2y = 4y - 22 + 5y$, then $y =$?

   A) -30

   B) $-4\frac{2}{3}$

   C) 14

   D) 30

4. Which of the following lists of numbers is in order from least to greatest?

   A) $\frac{1}{7}$, 0.125, $\frac{6}{9}$, 0.60

   B) $\frac{1}{7}$, 0.125, 0.60, $\frac{6}{9}$

   C) 0.125, $\frac{1}{7}$, 0.60, $\frac{6}{9}$

   D) $\frac{1}{7}$, 0.125, $\frac{6}{9}$, 0.60

5. Which of the following expressions is equivalent to $6x + 5 \geq -15 + 8x$?

   A) $x \leq -5$

   B) $x \leq 5$

   C) $x \leq 10$

   D) $x \leq 20$

6. Jane earns $15 per hour babysitting. If she starts out with $275 in her bank account, which of the following equations represents how many hours (h) she will have to babysit for her account to reach $400?

   A) $400 = 275 + 15h$

   B) $400 = 15h$

   C) $400 = \frac{15}{h} + 275$

   D) $400 = -275 - 15h$

7. At a bake sale, muffins are priced at $1.50 each and cookies are priced at $1 for two. If 11 muffins are sold, and the total money earned is $29.50, how many cookies were sold?

   A) 12

   B) 13

   C) 23

   D) 26

8. If $(2x + 6)(3x - 15) = 0$, then $x =$?

   A) $\{-5, 3\}$

   B) $\{-3, 5\}$

   C) $\{-2, -3\}$

   D) $\{-6, 15\}$

9. Adam is painting the outside of a 4-walled shed. The shed is 5 feet wide, 4 feet deep, and 7 feet high. How many square feet of paint will Adam need?

   A) 46

   B) 63

   C) 126

   D) 140

10. $4x + 3y = 10$

    $2x - y = 20$

    How many solutions (x, y) are there to the system of equations above?

    A) 0

    B) 1

    C) 2

    D) more than 2

11. $\frac{-6 + 11}{2(-3 - 8)} =$

    A) $-\frac{5}{22}$

    B) $-\frac{1}{2}$

    C) $\frac{5}{22}$

    D) $\frac{5}{9}$

12. $64 - 100x^2 =$

A) $(8 + 10x)(8 - 10x)$

B) $(8 + 10x)(8x + 10)$

C) $(8 - 10x)^2$

D) $(8 + 10x)^2$

13. A car dealership's commercials claim that this year's models are 20% off the list price, plus they will pay the first 3 monthly payments. If a car is listed for $26,580, and the monthly payments are set at $250, which of the following is the total potential savings?

A) $1,282

B) $5,566

C) $6,066

D) $20,514

14. A dry cleaner charges $3 per shirt, $6 per pair of pants, and an extra $5 per item for mending. Annie drops off 5 shirts and 4 pairs of pants, 2 of which need mending. Assuming the cleaner charges an 8% sales tax, which of the following will be the amount of Annie's total bill?

A) $45.08

B) $49.00

C) $52.92

D) $88.20

15. A sandwich shop earns $4 for every sandwich ($s$) it sells, $2 for every drink ($d$), and $1 for every cookie ($c$). If this is all the shop sells, which of the following equations represents what the shop's revenue (r) is over three days?

A) $r = 4s + 2d + 1c$

B) $r = 8s + 4d + 2c$

C) $r = 12s + 6d + 3c$

D) $r = 16s + 8d + 4c$

16. Which of the following is the y-intercept of the line whose equation is $7y - 42x + 7 = 0$?

A) $\left(\frac{1}{6}, 0\right)$

B) $(6, 0)$

C) $(0, -1)$

D) $(-1, 0)$

17. A rectangular field has area of 1452 square feet. If the width is three times greater than the length, which of the following is the length of the field?

A) 22 feet

B) 44 feet

C) 242 feet

D) 1452 feet

18. The owner of a newspaper has noticed that print subscriptions have gone down 40% while online subscriptions have gone up 60%. Print subscriptions once accounted for 70% of the newspaper's business, and online subscriptions accounted for 25%. Which of the following is the overall percentage growth or decline in business?

A) 13% decline

B) 15% decline

C) 28% growth

D) Business has stayed the same.

19. Based on a favorable performance review at work, Matt receives a $\frac{3}{20}$ increase in his hourly wage. If his original hourly wage is represented by w, which of the following represents his new wage?

A) $0.15w$

B) $0.85w$

C) $1.12w$

D) $1.15w$

COLLEGE LEVEL MATHEMATICS

1. The graph of which of the following equations is a straight line parallel to the graph of
   $3y - 1 = 2x$?

   A) $-3x + 2y = -2$

   B) $2x - 3y = 6$

   C) $-2x + 2y = 3$

   D) $-x + 3y = -2$

   E) $3x - 2y = 3$

2. If $16x^2 + 8x + 1 = 0$, then $x^3 = ?$

   A) $-\frac{1}{16}$

   B) $-\frac{1}{64}$

   C) 1

   D) 16

   E) 64

3. If $f(x) = x^2 + 3$ and $g(x) = 3x - 12$, then $f(g(5)) = ?$

   A) 12

   B) 28

   C) 32

   D) 72

   E) 78

4. What is an x-intercept of the graph $y = x^2 - 7x + 12$?

   A) -4

   B) 0

   C) 3

   D) 7

   E) 12

5. The sequence $\{a_n\}$ is defined by $a_1 = 5$ and $a_{n+1} = a_n + 7$ for $n = 1, 2, 3, \ldots$ What is the value of a_5?

   A) 12

   B) 20

   C) 26

   D) 30

   E) 33

6. What is the value of the expression $0.5^x + 1$ when $x = -2$?

   A) 0.75

   B) 1.25

   C) 2

   D) 4

   E) 5

7. Which of the following equations represents a line that passes through the points $(2, 7)$ and $(6, 10)$?

   A) $y = -\frac{3}{4}x + 5\frac{1}{2}$

   B) $y = -1\frac{1}{3}x - 4\frac{1}{2}$

   C) $y = \frac{3}{4}x + 5\frac{1}{2}$

   D) $y = \frac{4}{5}x - 5\frac{1}{2}$

   E) $y = 1\frac{1}{3}x + 2$

8. What is the value of the expression $|3x - y| + |2y - x|$ if $x = -4$ and $y = -1$?

   A) -13

   B) -11

   C) 11

   D) 13

   E) 24

9. $\dfrac{n!}{(n-2)!} =$

   A) $n(n - 1)$

   B) n

   C) $\dfrac{n}{n - 2}$

   D) n^2

   E) $\dfrac{n}{2}$

CONTINUE →

10. $m = 5^{-a}$

$m = 4^{-b}$

$m = 3^{-c}$

$m = 2^{-d}$

The variables a, b, c, and d each represent positive real numbers between 0 and 1. If m is a constant, which of the following expressions is true?

A) $a > b > c > d$

B) $b > a > c > d$

C) $c > d > b > a$

D) $d > c > b > a$

E) $a = b = c = d$

11. $\dfrac{(x^a y^b)(z^b y^a)}{z(xy)^a} =$

A) $y^b z^{(b-1)}$

B) $x y^b z^{(b-1)}$

C) $x y^{ab} z$

D) $\dfrac{y^b}{z^b}$

E) $\dfrac{x^{2a}}{z^{(b-1)}}$

12. As shown below, 2 identical circles are drawn next to each other with their sides just touching; both circles are enclosed in a rectangle whose sides are tangent to the circles. If each circle's radius is 2 centimeters, find the area of the rectangle.

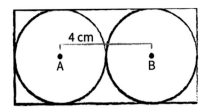

4 cm

A   B

A) 8 cm²

B) 16 cm²

C) 24 cm²

D) 30 cm²

E) 32 cm²

13. If $y = \log_3 x$, what is the value of y when $x = 81$?

A) 2

B) 4

C) 9

D) 27

E) 81

14. The county is instituting a new license plate system. The new plates will have 6 digits: the first digit will be 1, 2 or 3, and the next 5 digits can be any number from 0 – 9. How many possible unique combinations does this new system offer?

A) 53

B) 60

C) 3×10^5

D) 1×10^6

E) 3×10^6

15. John and Jake are working at a car wash. It takes John 1 hour to wash 3 cars; Jake can wash 3 cars in 45 minutes. If they work together, how many cars can they wash in 1 hour?

A) 6

B) 7

C) 9

D) 12

E) 13

16. Let $f(x) = 2x + 1$. If $g(x)$ is obtained by reflecting $f(x)$ across the y-axis and translating it 4 units in the positive y direction, what is $g(x)$?

A) $g(x) = -2x + 3$

B) $g(x) = -2x + 5$

C) $g(x) = 2x + 5$

D) $g(x) = 8x + 1$

E) $g(x) = 8x + 5$

17. The points $(-1, -1)$, $(-3, -8)$, $(0, 6)$ and $(5, 11)$ are plotted on a coordinate plane. How many of these 4 points are collinear with the points $(0, 1)$ and $(2, 5)$?

A) 0

B) 1

C) 2

D) 3

E) 4

18. If $m\beta < 90$ and $\cos\beta = \frac{\sqrt{3}}{2}$, then $\tan\beta = ?$

A) $-\sqrt{3}$

B) $\frac{-1}{\sqrt{3}}$

C) $\frac{1}{\sqrt{3}}$

D) 1

E) $\sqrt{3}$

19. $11, 7, 3, -1, \ldots$

If 11 is defined as the first term in the sequence given above, which of the following functions describes the sequence?

A) $f(n) = 11 + 4(n - 1)$

B) $f(n) = 11(4)^{(n-1)}$

C) $f(n) = 11 - 4n$

D) $f(n) = 15 - 4n$

E) $f(n) = 15 + 4(n + 1)$

20. A plane makes a trip of 246 miles. For some amount of time, the plane's speed is 115 miles per hour. For the remainder of the trip, the plane's speed is 250 miles per hour. If the total trip time is 72 minutes, how many minutes did the plane fly at 115 miles per hour?

A) 18

B) 23

C) 24

D) 28

E) 34

CONTINUE

READING COMPREHENSION

Directions for questions 1 – 12: Read the passage. Then choose the best answer to the question based on what you read.

1. It could be said that the great battle between the North and South we call the Civil War was a battle for individual identity. The states of the South had their own culture, one based on farming, independence, and the rights of both man and state to determine their own paths. Similarly, the North had forged its own identity as a center of centralized commerce and manufacturing. This clash of lifestyles was bound to create tension, and this tension was bound to lead to war. But people who try to sell you this narrative are wrong. The Civil War was a not a battle of cultural identities— it was a battle over slavery. All other explanations for the war are a either a direct consequence of the South's desire for wealth at the expense of her fellow man or a fanciful invention to cover up this sad portion of our nation's history. And it cannot be denied that this time in our past was very sad indeed.

    The main idea of the passage is that:

    A) The Civil War was the result of cultural differences between the North and South.

    B) The Civil War was the result of national division over slavery.

    C) The North's use of commerce and manufacturing allowed it to win the war.

    D) The South's belief in the rights of man and state cost them the war.

2. The most common way to measure body temperature is orally. A simple digital or disposable thermometer is placed under the tongue for a few minutes, and the task is complete. There are many situations, however, when measuring temperature orally isn't an option. For example, when a person cannot breathe through his nose, he won't be able to keep his mouth closed long enough to get an accurate reading. In these situations, it is often preferable to place the thermometer in the rectum or armpit. In fact, using the rectum provides a much more accurate reading than any other location does.

    When a person cannot breathe well, it is best to take his or her temperature—

    A) at a later time

    B) orally

    C) in the ear

    D) rectally

3. Although it's a common disease, the flu is actually not highly infectious; that is, it is relatively difficult to contract. The virus can only be transmitted when individuals come into direct contact with the bodily fluids of people infected with it, often when they are exposed to expelled aerosol particles resulting from coughing and sneezing. Since these particles only travel short distances and the virus will die within a few hours on hard surfaces, it can be contained with simple health measures like hand washing and face masks.

    The flu is not considered to be highly infectious because—

    A) Many people who get the flu will recover and have no lasting complications, so only a small number of people who become infected will die.

    B) The process of viral shedding takes two days, so infected individuals have enough time to implement simple health measures that stop the spread of the disease.

    C) The flu virus cannot travel far or live for long periods of time outside the human body, so its spread can easily be contained if measures are taken.

    D) Twenty-four hours is a relatively short period of time for the virus to spread among a population.

4. Mason was one of those guys who just always seemed at home. Stick him on a bus, and he'd make three new friends; when he joined a team, it was only a matter of time before he was elected captain. This particular skill rested almost entirely in his eyes. These brown orbs seemed lit from within, and when Mason focused that fire, it was impossible not to feel its warmth. People sought out Mason for the feeling of comfort he radiated, and

anyone with a good joke would want to tell it to him. His laughter started with a spark in his eyes that ignited into his wide smile.

Which of the following is a logical conclusion that can be drawn from this description?

A) Mason wishes people would tell him more jokes.

B) Mason is very good at sports.

C) Mason does not like when strangers approach him.

D) Mason has many friends.

5. Skin coloration and markings play an important role for snakes: they help snakes attract mates and warn predators that the snake is poisonous. However, those markings may be misleading. Some snakes have a found a way to ward off predators without the actual venom. The California king snake, for example, has very similar markings to the venomous coral snake with whom it frequently shares a habitat. But the king snake is actually nonvenomous; it's merely pretending to be dangerous to eat. A predatory hawk or eagle, usually hunting from high in the sky, can't tell the difference between the two species, so the king snake gets passed over and lives another day.

What can the reader conclude from the passage above?

A) The king snake is dangerous to humans.

B) The coral snake and the king snake are both hunted by the same predators.

C) It is safe to handle snakes in the woods because it is easy to determine whether they are poisonous.

D) The king snake changes its markings when hawks or eagles are close by.

6. Recently jazz has been associated with New Orleans, but in the 1920s jazz was a booming trend whose influence affected many aspects of American culture. During this time period, major urban centers like New York and Chicago experienced new economic, cultural, and artistic vitality. Jazz music was played by and for a more expressive and freed populace than the United States had previously seen. Jazz music also provided the soundtrack for the explosion of African American art and culture now known as the Harlem Renaissance, during which numerous musicians promoted their distinctive music

as an integral part of the emerging African American popular culture.

The main idea of the passage is that

A) People should associate jazz music with the 1920s, not modern New Orleans.

B) Many famous jazz musicians began their careers in New York City and Chicago.

C) African Americans were instrumental in launching jazz into mainstream culture.

D) Jazz music played an important role in many cultural movements of the 1920s.

7. Providing adequate nutrition to patients is one of the most important responsibilities of healthcare facilities. Patients, like all people, have two basic nutritional needs: they require macronutrients, the carbohydrates, fats, and proteins that provide energy; and micronutrients, which are the vitamins and elements the body needs to function properly. A good diet will provide the appropriate amount of macronutrients, or calories, to keep patients energized and satiated without leading to weight gain, while also providing necessary amounts of micronutrients. Such a diet will help patients remain comfortable and heal properly. A poor diet, on the other hand, can make recovery significantly more difficult.

According to the passage, the nutritional needs of patients in acute and long-term care facilities—

A) are always determined by a medical formula that combines an appropriate ratio of macronutrients and micronutrients

B) vary depending on the patient

C) do not significantly affect the recovery of the patient; medication is more important

D) do not significantly vary from patient to patient

8. Credit scores are used by many institutions to evaluate the risk of providing loans, rentals, or services to individuals. Banks use credit scores when deciding when to approve loans; they can also use them to determine the terms of the loan itself. Similarly, car dealers, landlords, and credit card companies will likely all access your credit report before agreeing to do business with you. Even your

employer can access a modified version of your credit report (although it will not have your actual credit score on it).

The main idea of the passage is that:

A) Credit scores are used by many different institutions for many different types of interactions with individuals.

B) Your credit report is not private information.

C) Credit scores may be used by many different institutions in business and financial transactions with individuals.

D) It is important to have a good credit score in order to secure a loan.

9. The American love affair with popcorn began in 1912, when it was first sold in theaters. The popcorn industry flourished during the Great Depression by advertising popcorn as a wholesome food that the poor could afford. With the introduction of mobile popcorn machines, popcorn moved from the theater into fairs and parks and continued to rule the snack food kingdom until the rise in popularity of home televisions during the 1950s.

It wasn't until microwave popcorn became commercially available in 1981 that at-home popcorn consumption began to grow exponentially. With the wide availability of microwaves in the United States, popcorn also began popping up in offices and hotel rooms. The home still remains the most popular popcorn eating spot, where Americans eat seventy percent of the sixteen billion quarts of popcorn consumed annually in the United States.

It can be concluded from the passage above that:

A) People ate less popcorn in the 1950s than in previous decades because they went to the movies less.

B) Without mobile popcorn machines, people would not have been able to eat popcorn during the Great Depression.

C) People enjoyed popcorn during the Great Depression because it was a luxury food.

D) During the 1800s, people began abandoning theaters to go to fairs and festivals.

10. The bacteria, fungi, insects, plants, and animals that live together in a habitat have developed complex interspecies interactions known as symbiotic relationships. Ecologists characterize these interactions based on whether each party benefits. In mutualism both individuals benefit, while in synnecrosis both organisms are harmed. A relationship in which one individual benefits and the other is harmed is known as parasitism. Examples of these relationships can easily be found in any ecosystem. Pollination, for example, is mutualistic—pollinators get nutrients from the flower, and the plant is able to reproduce—while tapeworms, which steal nutrients from their host, are parasitic.

The author's primary purpose in writing this essay is—

A) to describe different types of symbiotic relationships.

B) to argue that interspecies relationships are harmful.

C) to explain how competition for resources results in long-term interspecies relationships.

D) to provide examples of the many different types of interspecies interactions

12. In 1860, the United States was in a state of turmoil over slavery; the presidential election that year between Lincoln and Douglas reflected that issue. Lincoln was vehemently against slavery; Douglas spoke in favor of states' rights, which included a state's right to determine the legality of slavery independently of the federal government. Major legislation had placed restrictions on slavery in the west and then lifted them. These developments played a key role in the presidential campaigns of the two candidates. Lincoln and Douglas met around the country in a series of debates reflective of the national mood. Ultimately Lincoln was elected to the presidency; Southern Secession and the Civil War would soon follow.

According to this passage, the differences between Lincoln and Douglas

A) led to the presidential election of 1860.

B) illustrated the tensions and division in the United States before the Civil War.

C) were a reason for the major legislation—later overturned—that had placed restrictions on slavery in the west.

D) led to the Civil War.

11. Following more than three centuries under Portuguese rule, Brazil gained its independence in 1822, maintaining a monarchical system of government until the abolition of slavery in 1888 and the subsequent proclamation of a republic by the military in 1889. Brazilian coffee exporters politically dominated the country until populist leader Getulio Vargas rose to power in 1930. By far the largest and most populous country in South America, Brazil underwent more than a half century of populist and military government until 1985, when the military regime peacefully ceded power to civilian rulers. Brazil continues to pursue industrial and agricultural growth and development of its interior. Exploiting vast natural resources and a large labor pool, it is today South America's largest economy and a regional leader. Pressing problems include high income inequality, crime, inflation, rising unemployment, and corruption.

Courtesy CIA World Factbook 2015

It can be inferred from the passage that

A) Brazil is controlled by the military.

B) Brazil is a poor country.

C) coffee has historically been an important agricultural resource in Brazil.

D) Brazil was the last South American country to abolish slavery.

Directions for questions 13 – 22: Two sentences are shown and then followed by a question or a statement. Determine the best answer to the question or the best way to complete the statement.

13. Many young adults are seeking jobs that offer benefits such as health insurance.

   Some studies of people under twenty-eight show that these young adults value a high salary over health and retirement benefits.

   What does the underlined sentence do?

   A) It makes a contrast.

   B) It expands on the first sentence.

   C) It states an effect.

   D) It reinforces the first.

14. Yoga is a proven means of stress relief.

   In fact, it has been shown in scientific studies to reduce rates of heartburn, high blood pressure, and depression.

   What does the underlined sentence do?

   A) It makes a contrast.

   B) It proposes a solution.

   C) It gives an example.

   D) It analyzes the statement made in the first.

15. A poor credit report can make it difficult to get a reasonable mortgage or car loan.

   Fortunately, there are many options for credit repair, and it is possible to work with financial advisors to develop a plan to pay off loans and debts in order to improve your credit score.

   What does the underlined sentence do?

   A) It reinforces the first.

   B) It proposes a solution.

   C) It analyzes a statement made in the first.

   D) It makes a contrast.

CONTINUE →

16. Before the westward expansion of the United States, multitudes of buffalo—an important natural resource—roamed the Great Plains.

Enormous herds of buffalo migrated throughout the North American continent and supported the Native American tribes that dominated the terrain for centuries.

What does the underlined sentence do?

A) It states an effect.

B) It provides an example.

C) It proposes a solution.

D) It expands on the first sentence.

17. Young children require mental stimulation from an early age for their mental and behavioral growth.

Playing games and reading to small children helps with their cognitive development.

What does the underlined sentence do?

A) It draws a conclusion about what is stated in the first.

B) It makes a contrast.

C) It reinforces the first.

D) It proposes a solution.

18. An endangered species in the wild, pandas are supported and bred in zoos in their native China and elsewhere in the world.

Breeding programs have increased the panda population in captivity; Chinese, North American and European scientists collaborate in studying panda behavior to encourage breeding and population growth.

What does the underlined sentence do?

A) It states an effect.

B) It analyzes a statement in the first sentence.

C) It makes a contrast.

D) It expands on the first sentence.

19. Many teachers recommend that students study together in groups in order to practice quizzing each other on concepts and to discuss ideas and theories about which they may have questions.

Some students prefer to study alone because they find it difficult to focus on academic work in a group context, becoming distracted by discussions about social issues like sports and school events.

How do the two sentences relate?

A) They contradict each other.

B) They present a contrast.

C) They present a problem and a solution.

D) They present an argument and a supporting example.

20. More people are moving to Texas because of its strong economy, affordable housing, job opportunities, and limited state taxes.

In the fast-growing cities of Houston, Austin, and San Antonio, people are able to buy houses at more affordable rates than in cities like New York, Los Angeles or Chicago, making these Texas cities attractive destinations for young families.

How do the two sentences relate?

A) They establish a contrast.

B) They present a contradiction.

C) They reinforce each other.

D) They express roughly the same idea.

21. Many people work long hours and consequently eat too much processed or fast food, depriving them of adequate nutrition and providing them with too many empty calories instead.

Vitamin and mineral supplements are widely available at drugstores, and these products are usually very affordable; furthermore, there are multivitamins that contain essential minerals, so people need not take more than one capsule at a time.

How do the two sentences relate?

A) They present a problem and a solution.

B) They reinforce each other.

C) They express roughly the same idea.

D) They present a contradiction.

22. Many working Americans struggle with poverty despite having one or more jobs because their wages are not high enough to cover basic essentials like rent, food, and healthcare.

A higher minimum wage would allow more working Americans to improve their standard of living and ultimately save and invest money, strengthening the U.S. economy as a whole.

What does the second sentence do?

A) It proposes a solution.

B) It states an effect.

C) It makes a contrast.

D) It reinforces the first.

23. The social and political discourse of America continues to be permeated with idealism. An idealistic viewpoint asserts that the ideals of freedom, equality, justice, and human dignity are the truths that Americans must continue to aspire to. Idealists argue that truth is what should be, not necessarily what is. In general, they work to improve things and to make them as close to ideal as possible.

Which of the following best captures the author's purpose?

A) to advocate for freedom, equality, justice, and human rights

B) to explain what an idealist believes in

C) to explain what's wrong with social and political discourse in America

D) to persuade readers to believe in certain truths

The next four questions are based on this passage.

The best friend a man has in the world may turn against him and become his enemy. His son or daughter that he has reared with loving care may prove ungrateful. Those who are nearest and dearest to us, those whom we trust with our happiness and our good name may become traitors to their faith. The money that a man has, he may lose. It flies away from him, perhaps when he needs it most. A man's reputation may be sacrificed in a moment of ill-considered action.

The one absolutely unselfish friend that man can have in this selfish world, the one that never deserts him, the one that never proves ungrateful or treacherous is his dog. A man's dog stands by him in prosperity and in poverty, in health and in sickness. He will sleep on the cold ground, where the wintry winds blow and the snow drives fiercely, if only he may be near his master's side. He will kiss the hand that has no food to offer. He will lick the wounds and sores that come in encounters with the roughness of the world. He guards the sleep of his pauper master as if he were a prince. When all other friends desert, he remains.

George Graham Vest - c. 1855
http://www.historyplace.com/speeches/vest.htm

24. Which of the following best describes the structure of the text?

A) chronology

B) cause and effect

C) problem and solution

D) contrast

25. Which of the following could be considered the topic of this passage?

A) loyal friends

B) misfortune

C) human treachery

D) feeling safe

26. Which of the following is a logical conclusion of the passage?

A) Those closest to you will always betray you.

B) Friendships with other people are pointless.

C) Someone who wants a loyal friend should get a dog.

D) Only a dog can help a person through the rough times in his or her life.

⟶
CONTINUE

27. Which of the following is the purpose of this passage?

A) to inform

B) to entertain

C) to describe

D) to persuade

28. Examine the headings below. Based on the pattern, which of the following is a reasonable heading to insert in the blank spot?

> **Chapter 3: Planning Your Vacation**
>
> 1. Getting There
>   A. Air Travel
>   B. Traveling by Train
>   C. _____
>   D. Taking the Bus
> 2. Accommodations
> 3. Dining

A) Choosing a Destination

B) Navigating the Airport

C) Finding a Hotel

D) Road Trips

The next three questions are based on this passage.

Carl's Car Depot is hosting its one-day-only summer sale event! All sedans, trucks, SUVs, and more are marked to move quickly. We're offering no money down and low (like, really low) monthly payments. You won't find prices like these anywhere else in the city (or the state, or anywhere else you look). No matter what you're looking for, we've the new and used cars you need. We only drop our prices this low once a year, so don't miss out on this great deal!

29. Based on the context, which of the following is the meaning of the word *move* in the passage?

A) drive

B) sell

C) advance forward

D) change location

30. Which of the following best describes the author's purpose?

A) The author wants to tell customers what kinds of cars are available at Carl's Car Depot.

B) The author wants to encourage other car dealerships to lower their prices.

C) The author wants to provide new and used cars at affordable prices.

D) The author wants to attract customers to Carl's Car Depot.

31. Which of the following is NOT mentioned by the author as a reason to visit Carl's Car Depot?

A) They are offering lifetime warranties on new cars.

B) The sale will only last one day.

C) They have the lowest prices in town.

D) They are offering no money down and low monthly payments.

32. Although Ben *said* he supported for his coworkers, his actions suggested he did not condone their behavior.

Italics are used for which of the following reasons?

A) to show a word is intentionally misspelled

B) to indicate a word in a foreign language

C) to emphasize a contrast

D) to reference a footnote

SENTENCE SKILLS

Directions for questions 1 – 12: In the following questions, select the answer that best rewrites the underlined portion of the sentence. Note that the first answer choice indicates no change was made to the sentence.

1. Having finished her essay, <u>washing the truck was the thing Maricela was ready to do</u>.

   A) washing the truck was the thing Maricela was ready to do

   B) Maricela had another thing she was ready to do and that was washing the truck

   C) washing the truck Maricela was ready to do

   D) Maricela was ready to wash the truck

2. Many consider television <u>to be eroding of our nation's imaginations</u>.

   A) to be eroding of our nation's imaginations

   B) erosion of our nation's imaginations

   C) to erode our nation's imaginations

   D) to be eroding of the national imagination

3. <u>Hearing a lot in the news that</u> pet ownership is beneficial to health, especially for those with high blood pressure.

   A) Hearing a lot on the news that

   B) One often hears on the news that

   C) The news hears a lot that

   D) It is frequently heard in the news that

4. Raul, the most knowledgeable of us all, <u>maintain that we would be needing</u> better equipment.

   A) maintain that we would be needing

   B) maintains that we would be needing

   C) maintains that we would need

   D) maintain we would have needed

5. <u>Does anyone have a guess that they would like</u> to share before I reveal the answer?

   A) Does anyone have a guess that they would like

   B) Is anyone having a guess that they would like

   C) Do anyone have a guess that they would like

   D) Anyone with a guess would like

6. <u>The meals at this restaurant have so much more salt in them than the restaurant we went to last week.</u>

   A) The meals at this restaurant have so much more salt in them than the restaurant we went to last week.

   B) The meals at this restaurant are so much saltier than the restaurant we went to last week.

   C) The meals at this restaurant have so much more salt in them than that other restaurant.

   D) The meals at this restaurant have so much more salt in them than those at the restaurant we went to last week.

7. Even though she knew it would reflect badly, <u>the politician withdrawing her statement.</u>

   A) the politician withdrawing her statement

   B) the politician withdraws her statement

   C) the politician was going to withdraw her statement

   D) the politician withdrew her statement

8. The holiday Cinco de Mayo, a Mexican-American <u>tradition which celebrates the Mexican repulsion of the French occupation.</u>

   A) tradition which celebrates the Mexican repulsion of the French occupation

   B) tradition, celebrates the Mexican repulsion of the French occupation

   C) celebration of the Mexican repulsion of the French occupation

   D) celebrating of the Mexican repulsion of the French occupation

9. If you have <u>questions about the schedule, please be seeing your counselor</u>.

 A) questions about the schedule, please be seeing your counselor

 B) to ask the counselor your questions about the schedule

 C) questions about the schedule, please see your counselor

 D) a question about the schedule, be seeing your counselor

10. Tina and Marie <u>had never seen anyone eating so loud</u>.

 A) had never seen anyone eating so loud

 B) had never seen anyone eating so loudly

 C) never saw anyone eating so loud

 D) had never seen someone eating so loud

11. <u>It is so easy to be self-published these days; it seems as though everyone has a blog.</u>

 A) It is so easy to be self-published these days; it seems as though everyone has a blog.

 B) It is to easy to be self-published these days because it seems as though everyone has a blog.

 C) It is so easy to publish yourself these days; it seems as though everyone has a blog.

 D) It is so easy to be self-published these days; it seems as though everyone had a blog.

12. We reached the mountaintop and <u>was looking out at the view when the thunderstorm began</u>.

 A) was looking out at the view when the thunderstorm began

 B) were looking out at the incredible view when the thunderstorm began

 C) were in the middle of looking out at the view when the thunderstorm began

 D) were having looked out at the view when the thunderstorm began

Directions for questions 13 – 25: Select the answer that begins to rewrite the following sentences most effectively and without changing the meaning of the original sentence. Keep in mind that not every answer choice will complete the original sentence.

13. While shark attacks on humans are very rare, sometimes surfers look like seals on their boards, which can entice a passing shark.

 Rewrite, beginning with

 Shark attacks on humans are very rare,—

 The next words will be:

 A) but sometimes surfers

 B) and sometimes surfers

 C) even though sometimes surfers

 D) nevertheless sometimes surfers

14. The teacher saw no horseplay as he monitored the halls.

 Rewrite, beginning with:

 As he monitored the halls,—

 The next words will be:

 A) no horseplay could be seen.

 B) then the teacher saw no horseplay.

 C) and seeing no horseplay

 D) the teacher saw no horseplay.

15. It can be difficult to learn to play guitar, but the same cannot be said of the kazoo.

 Rewrite, beginning with:

 Unlike the kazoo,—

 The next words will be:

 A) it can be difficult to learn the guitar.

 B) we cannot easily learn the guitar.

 C) the guitar can be difficult to learn.

 D) the guitar is difficult to be learned.

16. The whistle was sounded, and the kickoff began.

Rewrite, beginning with:

The kickoff began—

The next words will be:

A) after the whistle was sounded.

B) and the whistle was sounded.

C) although the whistle was sounded.

D) the whistle was sounded.

17. Although the world of *Harry Potter* is filled with magic and wonder, issues such as classism exist even in that fictional world.

Rewrite, beginning with:

The world of Harry Potter *is filled with magic and wonder,—*

The next words will be:

A) but issues such as classism exist

B) nevertheless issues such as classism exist

C) and issues such as classism exist

D) even if issues such as classism exist

18. It is unusual to see wild orcas alone, since they are social animals.

Rewrite, beginning with:

Orcas are social animals,—

The next words will be:

A) so it is unusual to see them alone in the wild.

B) wild orcas are not usually seen alone.

C) and seeing wild orcas alone is unusual.

D) so it is alone that wild orcas are not seen.

19. The show began, and everyone shuffled to their seats.

Rewrite, beginning with:

Everyone shuffled to their seats—

The next words will be:

A) beginning the show.

B) when the show began.

C) although the show began.

D) and the show began.

20. If he needs help with his schoolwork, he will get a tutor.

Rewrite, beginning with:

He won't get a tutor—

The next words will be:

A) if he needs help.

B) when he needs help.

C) although he needs help.

D) unless he needs help.

21. If I had the resources, I would buy an energy-efficient car.

Rewrite, beginning with:

I cannot buy an energy-efficient car—

The next words will be:

A) when lacking the resources.

B) because I lack the resources.

C) although there are the resources.

D) without lacking the resources.

22. After twenty minutes of "debate," Talia felt weary of Jacob's stubbornness.

Rewrite, beginning with:

Talia felt weary of Jacob's stubbornness—

The next words will be:

A) "debating" him for twenty minutes.

B) having "debated" him for twenty minutes.

C) and they "debated" for twenty minutes.

D) despite having "debated" him for twenty minutes.

23. Tortoises have life expectancies of over 180 years, much longer than humans' life expectancies.

Rewrite, beginning with:

Unlike tortoises,—

The next words will be:

A) humans can live

B) humans do not live

C) it is not easy to live

D) long lives are difficult

24. Kelli felt excited and nervous when she moved into her first apartment.

Rewrite, beginning with:

Moving into her first apartment,—

The next words will be:

A) excitement and nervousness were felt by Kelli.

B) when Kelli felt excited and nervous.

C) Kelli felt excited and nervous.

D) Kelli feeling excited and nervous.

25. The music began to play, and everyone started to dance.

Rewrite, beginning with:

Everyone started to dance—

The next words will be:

A) and the music

B) before the music

C) after the music

D) although the music

WritePlacer

Write a multiple-paragraph essay of approximately 300 – 600 words based on the prompt below. Plan, write, review and edit your essay during the time provided, and read the prompt carefully before starting your essay.

Vaccines have been one of the most powerful and effective advances in modern medicine. Throughout most of our history, humans could do little to prevent the spread of disease. Now, we have the ability to create in most people an immunity to specific viruses and bacteria. Concerns about vaccines remain, however. Many people claim a religious objection to medical interference, while others worry about the safety of the young children being vaccinated. Scientists argue in return that allowing a few to opt out of vaccination endangers the whole community by making it possible for these diseases to return. Since personal freedom is such an important part of our culture, we must decide how to balance the safety of the community with the ability of citizens to make decisions about their own bodies and those of their children.

Write an essay of 300 – 600 words taking a position on whether vaccines should be mandatory. Support your position using logic and examples.

ESL – LANGUAGE USE

Fill in the blank in the sentence with the word or phrase that forms a grammatically correct sentence.

1. She told them to _____ their room before they left for the party.

   A) cleaned

   B) tidy

   C) clears

   D) neat

2. They left for the party, but Rebecca had to return home because _____ forgot her purse.

   A) he

   B) they

   C) we

   D) she

3. I had worked a very long shift, _____ I still had to run errands after work.

   Which conjunction best completes the sentence?

   A) and

   B) or

   C) but

   D) so

4. She hurried up that morning, _____ she wouldn't be late for her first day at work.

   Which word best completes the sentence?

   A) because

   B) for

   C) but

   D) so

5. _____ the Eiffel Tower when he visited Paris.

   Which of the following best completes the sentence?

   A) They saw

   B) He seen

   C) They seen

   D) He saw

Read the sentences and determine the best way to combine them.

6. With two bags to carry, Jim had a problem. His brother didn't have any.

   A) While his brother didn't have any, Jim had a problem with two bags to carry.

   B) With two bags to carry, Jim had a problem; his brother didn't have any.

   C) With two bags to carry, his brother didn't have any; Jim had a problem.

   D) Jim had a problem with two bags to carry because his brother didn't have any.

7. The mother was worried. Her daughter was out late.

   A) Even though her daughter was out late, the mother was worried.

   B) While the mother was worried, her daughter was out late.

   C) The mother was worried because her daughter was out late.

   D) Before the daughter was out late, her mother had been worried.

8. Brandon sighed as his car broke down. Jada tried to call a tow truck.

   A) Sighing as his car broke down, Jada tried to call a tow truck.

   B) Brandon sighed as his car broke down, so Jada tried to call a tow truck.

   C) Jada tried to call a tow truck, and Brandon sighed as his car broke down.

   D) While Brandon sighed as his car broke down and Jada tried to call a tow truck.

9. Kim and Hai took the dog for a walk. The dog chased a butterfly.

   A) When Kim and Hai took the dog for a walk, the dog chased a butterfly.

   B) The dog chased a butterfly as Kim and Hai had taken it for a walk.

   C) Kim and Hai took the dog for a walk because it had chased a butterfly.

   D) The dog chased a butterfly because Kim and Hai had taken it for a walk.

10. Laura liked to come home and relax. Her brother, however, expected her to cook dinner.

    A) Her brother expected her to cook, and Laura wanted to relax.

    B) Even though he expected her to cook dinner, Laura liked to relax.

    C) Coming home to relax, Laura's brother expected her to cook.

    D) Laura liked to come home and relax, but her brother expected her to cook dinner.

11. The parents were upset. The house was a mess, and the kids were still awake.

    A) The parents were upset and the house was a mess and the kids were still awake.

    B) The parents were upset because the house was a mess and the kids were still awake.

    C) The house was a mess and the kids were still awake because the parents were upset.

    D) When the parents were upset, the house was a mess and so the kids were still awake.

12. One key to a healthy diet is eating fruits and vegetables. Avoid drinking sugary sodas.

    A) Key to a healthy diet is eating fruits and vegetables and to avoid sugary sodas.

    B) Eating fruits and vegetables is key to a healthy diet, so sugary sodas should not be drunk.

    C) It is key to eat fruits and vegetables for a healthy diet, and to avoid sugary sodas.

    D) Avoiding sugary sodas and eating vegetables and fruits are the keys to a healthy diet.

13. The children went to the park. They played baseball with their friends.

    A) The children went to the park to play baseball with their friends.

    B) The children went to the park when they were playing baseball with their friends.

    C) To go to the park, the children played baseball with their friends.

    D) The children went to the park while they played baseball with their friends.

14. Many homeowners use natural cleaning products. They argue that natural ingredients are just as effective as industrial soaps.

    A) Arguing that natural ingredients are just as effective as industrial soaps, more homeowners are switching to natural products made up of these ingredients.

    B) Many homeowners prefer to use natural cleaning products, which they argue are just as effective as industrial soaps.

    C) Many natural products can be used for cleaning, but homeowners are using them instead of industrial soaps.

    D) Homeowners can use natural alternatives to industrial soaps, which they may no longer want to use.

15. Many people feel that the air conditioning in offices is too strong. However, it is difficult to get building managers to change the temperature.

    A) While it is difficult to get building managers to change the temperature, many people feel that office air conditioning is too strong.

    B) Even though many people feel that office air conditioning is too strong, it is difficult to get building managers to change the temperature.

    C) It is difficult to get building managers to change the temperature because many people feel that the air conditioning in offices is too strong.

    D) When people feel that office air conditioning is too strong, it is difficult to get building managers to change the temperature.

16. Wanda's car broke down. She had to call a tow truck.

    A) Wanda's car broke down because she had to call a tow truck.

    B) To call a tow truck, Wanda's car broke down.

    C) When Wanda's car broke down, she had to call a tow truck.

    D) Breaking down, Wanda's car had to call a tow truck.

17. Two raccoons live in that tree. They ate the vegetables in my garden.

  A) The two raccoons live in that tree when they ate the vegetables in my garden.

  B) Eating the vegetables in my garden, two raccoons live in that tree.

  C) Because they live in that tree, two raccoons ate the vegetables in my garden.

  D) The two raccoons that live in that tree ate the vegetables in my garden.

18. Gabriel needs to study. Luciana turns off the TV.

  A) Gabriel needs to study after Luciana turns off the TV.

  B) Luciana turns off the TV, so Gabriel needs to study.

  C) Because Gabriel needs to study, Luciana turns off the TV.

  D) Before Gabriel needs to study, Luciana turns off the TV.

Read the questions and select the best answer.

19. Which of the following sentences follows the rules of capitalization?

  A) As juveniles, african white-backed vultures are darkly colored, developing their white feathers only as they grow into adulthood.

  B) Ukrainians celebrate a holiday called *Malanka* during which men dress in costumes and masks and play tricks on their neighbors.

  C) Because of its distance from the sun, the planet neptune has seasons that last the equivalent of forty-one earth years.

  D) Edward Jenner, considered the Father of immunology, invented the world's first vaccine.

20. James had already been awake for nineteen hours___ after a twelve-hour work day, when he received the news.

  A) .

  B) ;

  C) ,

  D) —

21. Sandra's principal reason for choosing the job was that it would be full-time and would offer benefits.

  Which of the following is the complete subject in the sentence?

  A) Sandra's principal reason for choosing the job

  B) Sandra's principal reason

  C) Sandra's principal

  D) Sandra

22. First and foremost, they receive an <u>annual pension payment. The amount of the pension</u> has been reviewed and changed a number of times, most recently to reflect the salary of a high-level government executive.

  Which of the following would NOT be an acceptable way to revise and combine the underlined portion of the sentences above?

  A) annual pension payment, the amount of which

  B) annual pension payment; the amount of the pension

  C) annual pension payment; over the years since 1958, the amount of the pension

  D) annual pension payment, the amount of the pension

23. Which of the following sentences has the correct subject-verb agreement?

  A) The Akhal-Teke horse breed, originally from Turkmenistan, have long enjoyed a reputation for bravery and fortitude.

  B) The employer decided that he could not, due to the high cost of healthcare, afford to offer other benefits to his employees.

  C) Though Puerto Rico is known popularly for its beaches, its landscape also include mountains, which play home to many of the island's rural villages.

  D) Each of the storm chasers decide whether or not to go out when rain makes visibility low.

ESL – READING SKILLS

1. Many phone companies offer families annual group rates to save money on telephone, internet and text message charges. However, customers often complain about extra fees that cause their phone bills to be higher than they had expected. Citizens have complained to their government representatives about unfair marketing and trade practices by communications companies in this regard. As a result, some phone companies have begun to simplify their billing practices. In addition, smaller phone companies have emerged that offer prepaid or monthly plans with fewer fees and more straightforward charges.

   From this passage, which of these statements can the reader assume?

   A) Phone companies are breaking the law.

   B) Government involvement has forced phone companies to make changes.

   C) Customers should not have complained to the government.

   D) Small phone companies cannot afford to compete with big ones.

2. In the U.S., the states of the Great Plains include North and South Dakota, Nebraska, Kansas, and Oklahoma. Parts of eastern Montana, Wyoming, Colorado, and New Mexico also fall within the Great Plains, as does northwestern Texas. Historically the Great Plains were home to millions of buffalo, which were hunted by Native Americans. As the United States grew, the land was conquered and buffalo were killed, making way for white settlers who used the land for cattle ranching and eventually agriculture. Railroads allowed farmers to sell their crops in cities more easily. Today, many people have left the states of the Great Plains to pursue careers and livelihoods where opportunities in business and technology are more abundant in major cities elsewhere in the United States. However, new opportunities have appeared in Plains cities like Omaha and Oklahoma City and in the oil and gas industry in North Dakota.

   The Great Plains were originally—

   A) home to Native Americans and vast herds of buffalo

   B) settled by farmers and ranchers

   C) divided into five states

   D) a source of opportunities in business and technology

3. Roy and Leticia each work two jobs. Roy works for the water company as a technician and drives a taxi at night. Leticia is a medical assistant and takes care of her neighbor's children four nights a week, in addition to watching her own two sons. Once a week, Leticia goes to a medical class at the community college to improve her career opportunities. Both Roy and Leticia go to church on Sundays and participate in church activities on Sunday afternoons with their families.

   According to the passage, Leticia and Roy spend most of their time—

   A) working

   B) at church

   C) in medical class

   D) driving a taxi

4. Juan and his brother David own a business. Juan manages the money and works with clients, and David hires and manages the workers. Thanks to low taxes and high demand, their business is growing. Juan and David have both been able to buy houses for themselves and invest in better equipment for their business.

   From the passage, which of these statements can the reader assume?

   A) Juan and David do not work well together.

   B) David is not good at managing money.

   C) Juan is good at managing money.

   D) Juan is not good at managing people.

5. New York City can be a great place to raise a family. There are lots of parks and playgrounds for children, and plenty of good schools. It is easy for families of any income to get around on foot or using public

transportation. Moreover, New York has an abundance of cultural opportunities. With countless museums, galleries, theaters and musical performances year-round, it is one of the most diverse cities in the world.

An abundance of opportunities means—

A) limited opportunities

B) some opportunities

C) a lot of opportunities

D) a few opportunities

6. Jennifer is about to buy her first car. Since she drives every day, she wants a car that does not require a lot of gas or maintenance. Before going to look at cars, she spends several days researching different brands to find out which models are most reliable and efficient. She finally decides on three different types of cars that meet her needs and that she can afford. She plans to try driving each car to find out which one she is most comfortable driving.

Jennifer wants a car that does not need a lot of gas or maintenance because—

A) she drives every day

B) she does not have time to stop for gas every day

C) she is not comfortable with other models

D) she likes to do a lot of research

7. The Museum of Natural Science has opened an exhibit about the ecology of the Columbia River Basin. The exhibit includes plants, insects, birds, and mammals that are unique to the Columbia River Basin and explores the changes that have occurred in this delicate ecosystem over the last century. The exhibit has exciting audio-visual presentations. Individual tickets are available on the museum's website, and groups may apply for special ticket prices by calling the museum directly.

Which of the following is implied by the passage above?

A) The exhibit is about river ecosystems throughout North America.

B) The exhibit is very expensive for individuals.

C) The exhibit will not be open for very long.

D) The exhibit is interesting for visitors.

8. Today, school lunches consist of fried foods like french fries and chicken nuggets accompanied by defrosted vegetables that students often throw away. Many students drink sugary sodas or chocolate milk instead of water or calcium-rich, low-fat milk. Teachers and parents worry that children will grow up thinking that it is normal to eat these unhealthy meals every day. Furthermore, students in low-income families are particularly impacted by low-quality school food. Parents rely on schools to provide a warm, nutritious meal because they don't have the time or money to prepare food at home.

What is the main idea of this passage?

A) Many school lunches contain fried food.

B) Unhealthy school lunches pose a risk to students' long-term wellness, especially those students from low-income families.

C) Some families cannot afford to provide three warm meals a day and so rely on school lunches to help feed their children.

D) Unhealthy school lunches are a problem in many schools, especially those schools in low-income neighborhoods.

9. Football, or soccer as it is known in the United States, is probably the most popular sport in the world. Every four years, the World Cup brings together national football teams, even from countries that may historically be enemies or have bad political relationships. People put aside their differences to enjoy the exciting games and cheer on their national team. As teams are eliminated in games leading up to the final match, people around the globe take sides and support their favorite team as it plays for the ultimate prize: the FIFA World Cup Trophy.

The World Cup is played—

A) in the United States

B) only between countries that may be political rivals

C) every two years

D) every four years

10. Owning a cat is not difficult, but a few tips can help make life better for both you and your cat. First, it is a good idea to feed cats wet food twice a day; certain brands of wet cat food are especially high in protein, which is better for your cat's health than high-carbohydrate dry food. Second, be sure to clean your cat's litter box at least once a day. Otherwise, your cat may seek out another toilet in your home! In addition, be sure to take your pet for regular check-ups at the vet.

From this passage, which of these statements can the reader assume?

A) Cats prefer a clean living space.

B) Cats should not eat high-protein food.

C) Owning a cat is complicated and requires a lot of work.

D) Most people should not own cats.

11. Toussaint L'Ouverture was the leader of the Haitian Revolution, when slaves in Haiti rebelled against France, eventually winning their freedom and the independence of Haiti. L'Ouverture was a talented political and military leader, and he formed international alliances to support Haitian independence and freedom for the slaves. Although he died before independence was formally declared, his legacy continues as a fighter for justice and freedom.

What is the main idea of this passage?

A) Toussaint L'Ouverture was an important man.

B) Toussaint L'Ouverture was an important leader who fought for freedom in Haiti.

C) Toussaint L'Ouverture died before Haiti was formally independent.

D) Toussaint L'Ouverture was an important Haitian leader who formed alliances.

12. Some people enjoy giving presentations in front of a group, while others prefer to submit their work in a written document. These different approaches usually depend on an individual's personality. For example, a more outgoing person may enjoy capturing the attention of the crowd in a class or a meeting. In this case, he or she may wish to deliver a presentation about a recent project or assignment. On the other hand, someone who is shy or anxious about public speaking may feel uncomfortable standing up in front of a group of people. These individuals would rather spend more time writing up a report to submit to their teacher or supervisor instead of delivering a presentation in person.

An outgoing person—

A) is unlikely to be friendly with a shy person

B) is more likely to get a job than a shy person

C) is more likely to deliver a presentation than to write a report

D) is more likely to finish his or her work on time than a shy person

13. Many people enjoy the independence of owning and driving their own cars, but car ownership and commuting can become very expensive. In addition, driving in traffic is stressful and time-consuming. In order to save time and money, many people get to work or complete their daily tasks by carpooling, or sharing cars with their friends and co-workers. People take turns driving to work and other destinations, sharing the ride with their friends. This way, they can share fuel costs. Also, there is less traffic since there are fewer cars on the road.

The author of this passage probably assumes that:

A) Traffic problems are not important to many people.

B) It is hard for people to organize their schedules in order to carpool.

C) Carpooling is a bad idea.

D) Carpooling is a good idea.

CONTINUE

14. Many people love going into a store to do their shopping—trying on clothes, examining fruit, vegetables, and other goods, or talking to salespeople. However, more and more people do their shopping on the Internet. Online shopping saves time and is incredibly convenient; a variety of products are available at the click of a button. One drawback, however, is the cost of shipping. Store customers can bring their purchases home on the same day; online shoppers, however, must pay for shipping and wait for their purchases to be delivered.

    Drawback means:

    A) problem

    B) drawing

    C) cost

    D) expense

15. Nocturnal animals are animals that sleep during the day and are active at night. They may search for food, hunt, breed, fight, play, or do any other activity throughout the night, returning to their nests or lairs at sunrise to rest until sundown, when they come out again. Nocturnal animals are found throughout the United States and Canada and include bats, owls, certain species of cats, foxes, raccoons, possums, and more.

    What can the reader conclude from this passage?

    A) There are not many types of nocturnal animals.

    B) Nocturnal animals are relatively common.

    C) Nocturnal animals are relatively uncommon.

    D) Nocturnal animals are only found in the United States and Canada.

16. Niagara Falls is a popular destination for tourists. In the summer, tourists can take boats around the spectacular waterfall, and they can spend time exploring the local regions of upstate New York and southern Ontario. The city of Toronto is not far away. During the winter, sometimes the falls freeze over into enormous frozen icicles, amazing visitors. The falls rest right on the border between the United States and Canada, so tourists must remember to bring their passports if they wish to take advantage of all the attractions the region has to offer.

    According to the passage, Niagara Falls—

    A) is closed in the winter because it is frozen

    B) is only open in the summer because that is when tourists can visit it by boat

    C) is part of a larger region that is of interest to tourists

    D) is located in Canada

17. Chicago is the third-largest city in the United States. Located on the shores of Lake Michigan, Chicago is home to the Willis Tower, the tallest building in the U.S.; the Art Institute of Chicago, with world-renowned exhibitions; and Wrigley Field, home of the popular (if unlucky) Chicago Cubs, one of America's most famous baseball teams. Chicagoans enjoy cuisines from around the world. And, of course, any given night of the week music lovers can find great jazz and blues performers in the many clubs in this center of American music.

    It can be concluded from this passage that:

    A) Chicago is an interesting place to live and visit.

    B) It is difficult to find classical music concerts in Chicago.

    C) The Chicago Cubs will soon win the World Series.

    D) Jazz and blues are only played well in Chicago.

ESL – Sentence Meaning

Complete the sentence with the correct word or phrase.

1. During the 1950s, rock and roll music _____ very popular.

   A) become

   B) becoming

   C) became

   D) had became

2. Mai was _____ to her vacation.

   A) looking forward

   B) looking though

   C) looking at

   D) looking towards

3. Even though she is the _____ employee, Jessi finishes more projects than anyone else in the office.

   A) most new

   B) newer

   C) most newest

   D) newest

4. With majestic mountains, rolling prairies, breathtaking coastlines, and arctic expanses, the Canadian landscape _____ around the world for its beauty and diversity.

   A) are famous

   B) is famous

   C) famous

   D) were famous

5. Despite studying for hours, Carlos could not _____ the math assignment.

   A) figure out

   B) figure on

   C) figure around

   D) figure through

6. The children did not want to _____ their room after playing with all their toys.

   A) clean up

   B) clean over

   C) clear around

   D) clean off

7. Shawna is _____ than Alyssa at soccer, but Alyssa is a great basketball player.

   A) more good

   B) more better

   C) better

   D) the best

8. The water company plans to build a new pipe to bring water _____ the community, improving the service.

   A) from

   B) out of

   C) to

   D) on

Read the sentence(s), then answer the question.

9. The two men did not see eye to eye on how to finish the project.

   How did the men feel about the project?

   A) They agreed on how to finish it.

   B) They did not agree on how to finish it.

   C) They did not know how to finish it.

   D) They did not want to finish it.

10. Nadia had a good excuse for being late to class, so the teacher gave her the benefit of the doubt.

    How did the teacher feel about Nadia and her reason for being late?

    A) He was annoyed.

    B) He was confused.

    C) He did not trust her.

    D) He believed her.

11. The marble base gave the object a sense of permanence.

It seemed like the object would—

A) be there forever

B) be there for a short time

C) soon disappear

D) quickly fall over

12. Mrs. Gonzalez wouldn't be caught dead without her makeup on.

Mrs. Gonzalez—

A) will never die wearing her makeup

B) would never be seen without wearing makeup

C) would die before wearing makeup outside

D) is allergic to makeup

13. After a long day of work, Roger wanted to hit the sack.

Roger wanted to—

A) hit a bag

B) sit down

C) go to bed

D) put down his bag

14. Tyrese couldn't wait for his party.

Tyrese—

A) was very excited for his party

B) was too busy to have a party

C) had more important things to do than have a party

D) thought his party was planned too far in advance

15. Ron has two jobs, begins work at seven o'clock in the morning, and also takes classes online.

Which best describes Ron?

A) boring

B) caring

C) studious

D) hardworking

16. After their wedding, it looked like nothing but blue skies ahead for Sofia and Daniel.

Sofia and Daniel—

A) expected nice weather after their wedding

B) expected a positive future after their wedding

C) did not expect nice weather after their wedding

D) did not expect a positive future after their wedding

17. Christine and Daniella enjoy dancing, going to clubs, and parties.

Which best describes Christine and Daniella?

A) busy

B) fun-loving

C) friendly

D) lazy

18. Florida is a great place for a vacation: with family attractions, beautiful beaches, many flights from within the U.S., and reasonable hotels, it offers the best of both worlds.

Florida is a good place for a vacation because:

A) It is good for families and single people.

B) It has fun activities for children and adults.

C) It has all the advantages of an ideal destination.

D) It has two fun things to do.

19. Nicolas and Alexander had been friends for many years; their relationship was rock-solid.

Which best describes the boys' friendship?

A) It was very strong.

B) It was rocky.

C) It was at risk.

D) It was rigorous.

20. Janice does not beat around the bush at work, so her boss assigns her the most urgent projects.

Janice—

A) rushes through her work

B) works too quickly

C) does not work well with others

D) does not waste time at work

21. Rita always chooses what restaurant to visit with her friends—she will even try to order their food for them.

Rita is—

A) knowledgeable

B) bossy

C) friendly

D) outgoing

ANSWER KEY

Arithmetic

1.	A)	6.	D)	11.	A)	16.	C)
2.	B)	7.	C)	12.	B)	17.	D)
3.	C)	8.	A)	13.	D)	18.	C)
4.	C)	9.	C)	14.	B)	19.	D)
5.	D)	10.	C)	15.	B)		

Elementary Algebra

1.	D)	6.	A)	11.	A)	16.	C)
2.	C)	7.	D)	12.	A)	17.	A)
3.	C)	8.	B)	13.	C)	18.	A)
4.	C)	9.	C)	14.	C)	19.	D)
5.	C)	10.	B)	15.	A)		

College-Level Math

1.	B)	6.	E)	11.	A)	16.	B)
2.	B)	7.	C)	12.	E)	17.	C)
3.	A)	8.	D)	13.	B)	18.	C)
4.	C)	9.	A)	14.	C)	19.	D)
5.	E)	10.	D)	15.	B)	20.	C)

Reading Comprehension

1.	B)	9.	A)	17.	C)	25.	A)
2.	D)	10.	A)	18.	D)	26.	C)
3.	C)	11.	B)	19.	B)	27.	D)
4.	D)	12.	C)	20.	C)	28.	D)
5.	B)	13.	A)	21.	A)	29.	B)
6.	D)	14.	C)	22.	A)	30.	A)
7.	B)	15.	B)	23.	B)	31.	C)
8.	C)	16.	D)	24.	D)	32.	A)

Sentence Skills

1.	D)	8.	B)	15.	C)	22.	B)
2.	C)	9.	C)	16.	A)	23.	B)
3.	B)	10.	B)	17.	A)	24.	C)
4.	C)	11.	A)	18.	A)	25.	C)
5.	A)	12.	B)	19.	B)		
6.	D)	13.	A)	20.	D)		
7.	D)	14.	D)	21.	B)		

ESL – Language Use

1.	B)	7.	C)	13.	A)	19.	B)
2.	D)	8.	B)	14.	B)	20.	C)
3.	C)	9.	A)	15.	B)	21.	A)
4.	D)	10.	D)	16.	C)	22.	D)
5.	D)	11.	B)	17.	D)	23.	B)
6.	B)	12.	D)	18.	C)		

ESL – Reading Skills

1.	B)	6.	A)	11.	B)	16.	C)
2.	A)	7.	D)	12.	C)	17.	A)
3.	A)	8.	B)	13.	D)		
4.	C)	9.	D)	14.	A)		
5.	C)	10.	A)	15.	B)		

ESL – Sentence Meaning

1.	C)	7.	C)	13.	C)	19.	A)
2.	A)	8.	C)	14.	A)	20.	D)
3.	D)	9.	B)	15.	D)	21.	B)
4.	B)	10.	D)	16.	B)		
5.	A)	11.	A)	17.	B)		
6.	A)	12.	B)	18.	C)		

PRACTICE TEST TWO

ARITHMETIC

1. If the value of y is between 0.0047 and 0.0162, which of the following could be y?

A) 0.0035

B) 0.0055

C) 0.0185

D) 0.0238

2. $4\frac{1}{2} - 1\frac{2}{3} =$

A) $2\frac{1}{3}$

B) $2\frac{5}{6}$

C) $3\frac{1}{6}$

D) $3\frac{5}{6}$

3. $59.09 - 5.007 - 6.21 =$

A) 47.792

B) 47.81

C) 47.873

D) 47.882

4. 7 is what percent of 60?

A) 4.20

B) 8.57

C) 10.11

D) 11.67

5. $0.08 \times 0.12 =$

A) 0.0096

B) 0.096

C) 0.96

D) 9.6

6. Tiles are $12.51 per square yard. What will it cost to tile a room with if the room is 10 feet wide and 12 feet long?

A) $166.80

B) $178.70

C) $184.60

D) $190.90

7. $10\frac{3}{8} \div \frac{1}{3} =$

A) $3\frac{13}{24}$

B) $6\frac{3}{4}$

C) $15\frac{3}{4}$

D) $31\frac{1}{8}$

8. A car dealership has sedans, SUVs, and minivans in a ratio of 6:3:1, respectively. What proportion of the vehicles at the dealership are sedans?

A) $\frac{1}{6}$

B) $\frac{3}{10}$

C) $\frac{1}{2}$

D) $\frac{3}{5}$

9. If there are 380 female students in a class, and male students make up 60% of the class, how many total students are in the class?

A) 570

B) 633

C) 950

D) 2280

10. $4 - \frac{1}{2^2} + 24 \div (8 + 12) =$

A) 1.39

B) 2.74

C) 4.95

D) 15.28

11. Dora commutes to work every day. During the week, her commute times were 29.15 minutes, 30.75 minutes, 28.59 minutes, 27.20 minutes, and 35.62 minutes. If the times are rounded to nearest minute, which is the best estimate of the total time Dora spent on her commute during this week?

A) 149

B) 150

C) 151

D) 152

12. What is 18 percent of 11,400?

A) 633

B) 2052

C) 3553

D) 8700

13. What is $\frac{1587}{98}$ rounded to the nearest integer?

A) 15

B) 16

C) 17

D) 18

14. A marinade recipe calls for 2 tablespoons of lemon juice for $\frac{1}{4}$ cup of olive oil. How many tablespoons of lemon juice would be used with $\frac{2}{3}$ cup olive oil?

A) $\frac{3}{4}$

B) $2\frac{1}{3}$

C) 4

D) $5\frac{1}{3}$

15. How many digits are in the sum 951.4 + 98.908 + 1.053?

A) 4

B) 5

C) 6

D) 7

16. $105.71 \div 31 =$

A) 0.341

B) 3.41

C) 34.1

D) 341

17. Which of the following is the least?

A) 1.068

B) 1.680

C) 1.608

D) 1.086

18. $5\frac{2}{3} \times 1\frac{7}{8} \div \frac{1}{3}$

Simplify the expression. Which of the following is correct?

A. $3\frac{13}{24}$

B. $6\frac{3}{4}$

C. $15\frac{3}{4}$

D. $31\frac{7}{8}$

ELEMENTARY ALGEBRA

1. Which expression is equivalent to
$2(-3x - 2) < 2$?

   A) $x > -2$

   B) $x < -\frac{2}{3}$

   C) $x < -1$

   D) $x > -1$

2. $x^3 - 3x^2 + (2x)^3 - x =$

   A) $20x$

   B) $x^3 - 3x^2 + 7x$

   C) $7x^3 - 3x^2 - x$

   D) $9x^3 - 3x^2 - x$

3. What is the value of the expression $\frac{4x}{x-1}$ when $x = 5$?

   A) 3

   B) 4

   C) 5

   D) 6

4. If $3a + 4 = 2a$, then $a = ?$

   A) -4

   B) $-\frac{4}{5}$

   C) $\frac{4}{5}$

   D) 4

5. Which of the following lists of numbers is in order from least to greatest?

   A) $\frac{1}{24} < \frac{3}{32} < \frac{5}{48} < \frac{2}{16} < \frac{3}{16}$

   B) $\frac{1}{24} < \frac{5}{48} < \frac{3}{32} < \frac{2}{16} < \frac{3}{16}$

   C) $\frac{1}{24} < \frac{3}{32} < \frac{2}{16} < \frac{3}{16} < \frac{5}{48}$

   D) $\frac{1}{24} < \frac{2}{16} < \frac{3}{32} < \frac{3}{16} < \frac{5}{48}$

6. A cleaning company charges $25 per hour per room. A 7% sales tax is added to this charge. If t represents the number of hours and r represents the number of rooms, which of the following algebraic equations represents the total cost c of cleaning?

   A) $c = 25.07(t)(r)$

   B) $c = 32.00(t)(r)$

   C) $c = 26.75(t)(r)$

   D) $c = \frac{26.75(t)}{(r)}$

7. For which of the following expressions are $x = 3$ and $x = -2$ both solutions?

   A) $x^2 - x - 6$

   B) $x^2 - x + 6$

   C) $x^2 + x - 6$

   D) $x^2 + x + 6$

8. $100x^2 + 25x =$

   A) $25(4x + x)$

   B) $25(4x^2 + x)$

   C) $25x(4x + 1)$

   D) $100x(x + 25x)$

9. If m represents a car's average mileage in miles per gallon, p represents the price of gas in dollars per gallon, and d represents a distance in miles, which of the following algebraic equations represents the cost (c) of gas per mile?

   A) $c = \frac{dp}{m}$

   B) $c = \frac{p}{m}$

   C) $c = \frac{mp}{d}$

   D) $c = \frac{m}{p}$

10. If $y = |x - 28|$, what is the value of y when $x = 12$?

   A) -40

   B) -16

   C) 16

   D) 40

11. Melissa is ordering fencing to enclose an area of 5625 square feet in the shape of a square. How many feet of fencing does she need?

    A) 75

    B) 150

    C) 300

    D) 5,625

12. $\frac{21x^4 + 14x^2}{7x} =$

    A) $3x^3 + 2x$

    B) $3x^5 + 2x^3$

    C) $\frac{3x^4 + 2x}{x}$

    D) $\frac{3x^3 + 2x}{7}$

13. A restaurant employs servers, hosts, and managers in a ratio of 9:2:1. If there are 36 total employees, which of the following is the number of hosts at the restaurant?

    A) 3

    B) 4

    C) 6

    D) 8

14. If x is the proportion of men who play an instrument, y is the proportion of women who play an instrument, and z is the total number of men, which of the following is true?

    A. $\frac{z}{x}$ = number of men who play an instrument

    B. $(1 - z)x$ = number of men who do not play an instrument

    C. $(1 - x)z$ = number of men who do not play an instrument

    D. $(1 - y)z$ = number of women who do not play an instrument

15. A woman's dinner bill comes to $48.30. If she adds a 20% tip, which of the following will be her total bill?

    A) $9.66

    B) $38.64

    C) $48.30

    D) $57.96

16. Which of the following lists is in order from least to greatest?

    A) $\frac{1}{7}$, 0.125, $\frac{6}{9}$, 0.60

    B) $\frac{1}{7}$, 0.125, 0.60, $\frac{6}{9}$

    C) 0.125, $\frac{1}{7}$, 0.60, $\frac{6}{9}$

    D) 0.125, $\frac{1}{7}$, 0.125, $\frac{6}{9}$, 0.60

17. Which of the following is equivalent to 3.28?

    A) $3\frac{1}{50}$

    B) $3\frac{1}{25}$

    C) $3\frac{7}{50}$

    D) $3\frac{7}{25}$

18. $x \div 7 = x - 36$

    Solve the equation. Which of the following is correct?

    A) $x = 6$

    B) $x = 42$

    C) $x = 126$

    D) $x = 252$

19. After taxes, a worker earned $15,036 in 7 months. Which of the following is the amount the worker earned in 2 months?

    A) $2,148

    B) $4,296

    C) $6,444

    D) $8,592

20. $\frac{4x - 5}{3} = \frac{\frac{1}{2}(2x - 6)}{5}$

    Simplify the expression. Which of the following is the value of x?

    A) $-\frac{2}{7}$

    B) $-\frac{4}{17}$

    C) $\frac{16}{17}$

    D) $\frac{8}{7}$

COLLEGE-LEVEL MATH

1. Sequence $\{a_n\}$ is defined as $a_n = 11, 7, 3, -1, \ldots$ where $a_1 = 11$. Which expression defines a_n?

   A) $a_n = 11 + 4(n-1)$

   B) $a_n = 11(4)^{(n-1)}$

   C) $a_n = 11 - 4n$

   D) $a_n = 15 - 4n$

   E) $a_n = 15 + 4(n-1)$

2. $3a^2 - 11a + 10 = 0$

   What is the sum of all the values of a that satisfy the equation above?

   A) 3

   B) 7

   C) 13

   D) 15

   E) 30

3. For which of the following functions does $f(x) = |f(x)|$ for every value of x?

   A) $f(x) = x^{\frac{1}{3}}$

   B) $f(x) = 3 - x$

   C) $f(x) = 2x + x^2$

   D) $f(x) = x^3 + 1$

   E) $f(x) = x^2 + (2-x)^2$

4. If $f(x) = 3^x - 2$, what is the value of $f(5)$?

   A) 13

   B) 27

   C) 241

   D) 243

   E) 727

5. $|3x - 5| = 23$

   $|10 + 4y| = 12$

   If x and y are both negative numbers in the system of equations above, what is $|y - x|$?

   A) 0.5

   B) 4

   C) 7.33

   D) 8

   E) 8.5

6. If $y = \log_x 64$, what is the value of y when $x = 4$?

   A) $\frac{1}{2}$

   B) $\frac{1}{3}$

   C) 2

   D) 3

   E) 16

7. A root of $x^2 + 7x = -8$ is

   A) -8

   B) $-7 + \sqrt{\frac{17}{2}}$

   C) $-7 + \sqrt{\frac{41}{2}}$

   D) 1

   E) $7 - \sqrt{\frac{17}{2}}$

8. If $f(x) = 8x + 2$ and $g(x) = x + \frac{6}{8}$, then $f(g(x)) =$

   A) $x + 1$

   B) $x + 8$

   C) $x + 6$

   D) $8x + 8$

   E) $8x + 50$

9. A radio station plays songs that last an average of 3.5 minutes and has commercial breaks that last 2 minutes. If the station is required to play 1 commercial break for every 4 songs, how many songs can the station play in an hour?

   A) 14

   B) 15

   C) 16

   D) 17

   E) 18

10. If $\frac{x}{7} = x - 36$, then $\left(\frac{x}{2}\right)^2 =$

    A) 5.0625

    B) 9

    C) 441

    D) 20,736

    E) 15,876

11. What is the surface area of a box that is 12 inches long, 18 inches wide, and 6 inches high?

    A) 144 in^2

    B) 396 in^2

    C) 412 in^2

    D) 792 in^2

    E) 1,296 in^2

12. The graph of which of the following equations is a straight line perpendicular to the graph of $y = 2.5x - 3$?

    A) $y = -0.4 + 2.5$

    B) $y = -2.5 + 0.4$

    C) $y = 0.33 + 0.4$

    D) $y = 0.33 + .04$

    E) $y = 0.4 + 2.5$

13. Out of 7 students, 3 will be chosen to represent the school at a city council meeting. How many different groups of 3 students can be chosen?

    A) 21

    B) 27

    C) 35

    D) 210

    E) 343

14. The area of a right triangle is 24.5 square centimeters. If one of its angles measures 45°, what is the length of its hypotenuse in centimeters?

    A) 7

    B) 8.9

    C) 9.9

    D) 10

    E) 17.3

15. $(5 + \sqrt{5})(5 - \sqrt{5}) =$

    A) $10\sqrt{5}$

    B) 20

    C) 25

    D) $25\sqrt{5}$

    E) $25 - 2\sqrt{5}$

16. A painting is leaning against a wall. If the painting is 20 inches tall and forms a 20° angle with the wall, how many inches is the base of the painting from the wall?

    A) 6.8

    B) 7.3

    C) 8.2

    D) 18.8

    E) 58.5

17. A circle and line are plotted on the same coordinate plane. What is the maximum number of points at which the circle and line can intersect?

    A) 0

    B) 1

    C) 2

    D) 3

    E) More than 3

18. A chemical experiment requires that a solute be diluted with 4 parts (by mass) water for every 1 part (by mass) solute. If the desired mass for the solution is 90 grams, how many grams of solute should be used?

    A) 15

    B) 16.5

    C) 18

    D) 22.5

    E) 72

19. $3a(4a + 6) - (2a - 4) =$

    A) $-(12a + 1)(a + 1)$

    B) $(12a - 1)(a - 1)$

    C) $(12a + 4)(a - 1)$

    D) $(12a - 4)(a + 1)$

    E) $(12a + 4)(a + 1)$

20. If $x^2 - 9 < 0$, what are all the possible values of x?

    A) $x > 3$ or $x < -3$

    B) $-3 < x < 3$

    C) $x > 3$

    D) $x < -3$

    E) $x < 9$

READING COMPREHENSION

Directions for questions 1 – 12: Read the passage. Then choose the best answer to the question based on what you read.

1. For centuries China stood as a leading civilization, outpacing the rest of the world in the arts and sciences, but in the nineteenth and early twentieth centuries, the country was beset by civil unrest, major famines, military defeats, and foreign occupation. After World War II, the communists under Mao Zedong established an autocratic socialist system that, while ensuring China's sovereignty, imposed strict controls over everyday life and cost the lives of tens of millions of people. After 1978, Mao's successor Deng Xiaoping and other leaders focused on market-oriented economic development and by 2000 output had quadrupled. For much of the population, living standards have improved dramatically and the room for personal choice has expanded, yet political controls remain tight. Since the early 1990s, China has increased its global outreach and participation in international organizations.

   Courtesy CIA World Factbook, 2015

   Following the rule of Mao Zedong, China's economy—

   A) faltered due to continuing tight political controls

   B) developed rapidly after moving to a market-based model

   C) developed into an autocratic socialist system that imposed strict controls over everyday life

   D) helped the country become a leading global civilization

2. Providing students with their own laptop or tablet will allow them to explore new programs and software in class with teachers and classmates and to practice using it at home. In schools without laptops for students, classes have to visit computer labs where they share old computers often missing keys or that run so slowly they are hardly powered on before class ends. When a teacher tries to show students how to use a new tool or website, students must scramble to follow along and have no time to explore the new feature. If they can take laptops home instead, students can do things like practice editing video clips or photographs until they are perfect. They can email classmates or use shared files to collaborate even after school. If schools expect students to learn these skills, it is the schools' responsibility to provide students with enough opportunities to practice them.

   The author's purpose in writing this passage is to

   A) teach high school students how to use computers properly.

   B) describe the ways that schools make technology available to students today.

   C) argue that schools should make computer technology available to students.

   D) illustrate the benefits of technology in academics.

3. The Americas were quickly colonized by Europeans after Christopher Columbus first laid claim to them for the Spanish, and the British, French and Spanish all held territories in North America throughout the sixteenth, seventeenth, eighteenth and nineteenth centuries. The British ultimately controlled most of the

   Atlantic coast and some territories inland—what became known as the Thirteen Colonies—while France controlled most of what is today Quebec, the Midwest, and the Mississippi River Valley region. Spain's holdings extended through Mexico into Texas, the Southwest, and eventually California, reaching as far north into what are today parts of Montana and Wyoming, in addition to Florida. The Northeast and

   Upper Midwest were rich in game and beaver pelts, and the areas on the mid-Atlantic coast were agriculturally fertile. They also contained important commercial centers like New York, Boston and Philadelphia where North American products went to port.

   It could be concluded from this passage that European powers were interested in colonizing North America because

→

CONTINUE

A) North America was rich in land and profitable natural resources; furthermore, coastal settlements allowed these products to be easily shipped overseas.

B) France and Britain wanted to compete with Spain for resources in the Western Hemisphere.

C) Christopher Columbus' initial voyages made it safer for other explorers to lay claim to inland territory.

D) the large amount of land made it possible for Britain, France and Spain to split territory equitably.

4. Meteorologists study the climate of an area, its typical weather pattern over an extended period of time. For example, much of the United States experiences a four-season cycle, or temperate climate, while Central Africa, Southeast Asia and parts of Central and South America (located between the Tropic of Cancer and the Tropic of Capricorn) have tropical climates, characterized by high humidity. Climates can determine the nature of land: a desert is an area where there is little precipitation, or rain, resulting in limited vegetation and infertile land. In the hydrologic cycle, water circulates between the land, the atmosphere, and the hydrosphere, or bodies of water on the Earth. Storms like hurricanes, found in the tropical West Atlantic Ocean and the Caribbean Sea, typhoons, in the western Pacific, and cyclones in the Indian Ocean, are all major storms with winds that reach speeds of at least seventy-four miles per hour.

Major storms like hurricanes, typhoons and cyclones are distinguished by

A) appearing as part of the hydrologic cycle.

B) winds with speeds of at least seventy-five miles per hour.

C) winds with speeds of at least seventy-four miles per hour.

D) winds with speeds up to seventy-four miles per hour.

5. Major tenets of Hindu belief include reincarnation, or that the universe and its beings undergo endless cycles of rebirth and karma, that one creates one's own destiny. The soul is reincarnated until it has resolved all karmas, at which point it attains moksha, or liberation from the cycle. Hindus believe in multiple divine beings. The religion is based in the Vedic scriptures; other important texts include the Upanishads, the Mahabharata, and the Bhagavad Gita. Hinduism is the primary religion in India and is intertwined with the caste system, the hierarchical societal structure.

The purpose of this passage is to present

A) a comparison of Hindu religion and social structure.

B) a description of reincarnation.

C) a listing of important Hindu literature.

D) a brief overview of Hinduism and its main precepts.

6. It's easy to puzzle over the landscapes of our solar system's distant planets—how could we ever know what those far-flung places really look like? However, scientists utilize a number of tools to visualize the surfaces of many planets. The topography of Venus, for example, has been explored by several space probes, including the Russian Venera landers and NASA's Magellan orbiter. These craft used imaging and radar to map the surface of the planet, identifying a whole host of features including volcanoes, craters, and a complex system of channels. Mars has likewise been mapped by space probes, including the famous Mars Rovers, which are automated vehicles that actually landed on the planet's surface. These rovers have been used by NASA and other space agencies to study the geology, climate, and possible biology of the planet.

In addition to these long-range probes, NASA has also used its series of orbiting telescopes to study distant planets. These four massively powerful telescopes include the famous Hubble Space Telescope as well as the Compton Gamma Ray Observatory, Chandra X-Ray Observatory, and the Spitzer Space Telescope. These allow scientists to examine planets using not only visible light but also infrared and near-infrared light, ultraviolet light, x-rays and gamma rays.

Powerful telescopes aren't just found in space: NASA makes use of Earth-bound telescopes as well. Scientists at the National Radio Astronomy Observatory in Charlottesville, VA, have spent decades using radio imaging to build an incredibly detailed portrait of Venus' surface. In fact, Earth-bound telescopes offer a distinct advantage over orbiting telescopes because they allow scientists to capture data from a fixed point, which in turn allows them to effectively compare data collected over long period of time.

Which of the following sentences best describes the main idea of the passage?

A) It's impossible to know what the surfaces of other planets are really like.

B) Telescopes are an important tool for scientists studying planets in our solar system.

C) Venus' surface has many of the same features as the Earth's, including volcanoes, craters, and channels.

D) Scientists use a variety of advanced technologies to study the surface of the planets in our solar system.

7. The U.S. Constitution is a single document codifying the foundational laws of the country. It provides for a federal government, but one that is based on popular sovereignty, separation of powers, limited government and checks and balances in order to protect from federal overreach. Popular sovereignty meant that government can only exist with the consent of the governed. One important example of protection of that consent in the Constitution is habeas corpus, according to which the government cannot detain a person indefinitely without charges. The three articles of the Constitution laid out a framework for a limited federal government, including a separation of powers between the legislative (Article I), executive (Article II), and judicial (Article III) branches. Each of these branches has the ability to check, or limit, the powers of the others. Powers held by more than one branch of government are called concurrent powers.

The purpose of the three branches of government is to

A) ensure that each branch of government is limited in its powers by the other two—a system of checks and balances.

B) ensure that each branch of government is limited in its powers by the other two—a system of popular sovereignty.

C) ensure that government can only exist with the consent of the governed.

D) protect the rule of habeas corpus.

8. Exercise is critical for healthy development in children. Today, there is an epidemic of unhealthy children in the United States who will face health problems in adulthood due to poor diet and lack of exercise in childhood. This is a problem for all Americans, especially with the rising cost of healthcare.

It is vital that school systems and parents encourage their children to engage in a minimum of thirty minutes of cardiovascular exercise each day, mildly increasing their heart rate for a sustained period. This is proven to decrease the likelihood of developmental diabetes, obesity, and a multitude of other health problems. Also, children need a proper diet rich in fruits and vegetables so that they can grow and develop physically, as well as learn healthy eating habits early on.

Parents and schools are responsible for

A) covering the rising cost of healthcare in the United States today.

B) getting thirty minutes of cardiovascular exercise per day and eating nutritious meals.

C) decreasing the likelihood of developmental diabetes, obesity, and other problems.

D) ensuring that children get at least thirty minutes of exercise per day and receive nutritious meals.

9. The issue of public transportation has begun to haunt the fast-growing cities of the southern United States. Cities like Atlanta, Dallas, and Houston are full of sprawling suburbs and single-family homes, not densely concentrated skyscrapers and apartments. Highways are the twenty-lane-wide expanses of concrete that allow commuters to move from home to work and back again. But these modern miracles have become time-sucking, pollution-spewing nightmares. It's time for these cities to adopt public transport like trains and buses if they are to remain livable.

This passage implies that

→ CONTINUE

A) cities in the southern United States are growing more rapidly than anywhere else in the nation.

B) public transportation is too difficult to integrate into cities like Atlanta, Dallas, and Houston, which are dependent on cars and highways.

C) Atlanta, Dallas and Houston do not currently have strong public transportation systems.

D) highways are modern miracles.

10. The explorations of European sailors and their patrons in the fifteenth century were not the result of a desire to discover new lands, but rather to discover better trade routes and spread European culture and the Christian religion. They were, at this time, particularly interested in South and East Asia, relatively untouched by earlier Christian missionaries and difficult to access for traders. The desire to convert new Christians was especially pressing for the Catholic Church in the face of the Protestant Reformation, which began at the very end of the fifteenth century.

According to the passage, European exploration in the fifteenth century focused on

A) the discovery of new lands, such as those found in the Western Hemisphere.

B) spreading the Protestant Reformation.

C) finding better trade routes and spreading Christianity.

D) finding better trade routes only.

11. A land of vast distances and rich natural resources, Canada became a self-governing dominion in 1867, while retaining ties to the British crown. Economically and technologically, the nation has developed in parallel with the US, its neighbor to the south across the world's longest unfortified border. Canada faces the political challenges of meeting public demands for quality improvements in health care, education, social services, and economic competitiveness, as well as responding to the particular concerns of predominantly francophone Quebec. Canada also aims to develop its diverse energy resources while maintaining its commitment to the environment.

Courtesy CIA World Factbook 2015

The passage implies that

A) Canada remains under the control of Great Britain.

B) Canada and the United States have a strong and positive relationship.

C) Canada has developed thanks to support from the United States.

D) Canada is unable to meet many of the political challenges with which it is faced.

12. Language branches are built on actual, documented languages that evolved from an ancient ancestor language no longer spoken today. Latin is the basis of a language branch. You may, for instance, find it relatively easy to understand Italian if you can speak Spanish, because they are both based in Latin, the now-dead language of the Roman Empire; however, but they are distinct languages with their own rules, grammar and vocabulary.

A language group encompasses all the living languages that are part of a language branch. The languages that evolved out of Latin, including Spanish and Italian, are called the Romance languages. The individual languages have their own dialects and accents. Similar languages may share some vocabulary or grammar; while some words or usages may differ, if you can speak a language, you can understand a regional dialect (perhaps with some difficulty).

The purpose of this passage is to explain

A) the technical methods linguists use to organize and classify languages.

B) how languages are related based on the ancestry they share.

C) why Spanish and Italian sound similar.

D) why a Spanish-speaking person can learn Italian easily.

Directions for questions 13 – 22: Two sentences are shown and then followed by a question or a statement. Determine the best answer to the question or the best way to complete the statement.

13. High heat and humidity can trigger asthma attacks in children and the elderly.

    Providing air conditioning can significantly reduce the risk of asthma attacks in these vulnerable populations during hot and humid days; recent studies have proved this in Louisiana and Florida.

    What does the underlined sentence do?

    A) It states an effect.

    B) It proposes a solution.

    C) It gives an example.

    D) It analyzes the statement made in the first.

14. Alligators look heavy and slow, but they can move very quickly; in Florida and the Gulf Coast of the United States, it is important to be cautious in areas where alligators live.

    There are increasing reports of alligators being discovered in homeowners' backyards as housing developments expand into alligator habitats; upsetting stories of alligator attacks on pets are not unheard of.

    What does the underlined sentence do?

    A) It makes a contrast.

    B) It expands on the first sentence.

    C) It states an effect.

    D) It reinforces the first.

15. Mountain climbing is a popular sport around the world; thanks to expeditionary companies, more people than ever before are able to try to climb the highest mountains on every continent and enjoy this exciting activity.

    Mountain climbing is a popular but risky sport; untrained climbers pose a risk to themselves and to others when they try to climb peaks that are too difficult for them, and expeditionary companies act unprofessionally when they encourage this.

What does the underlined sentence do?

A) It reinforces the first.

B) It proposes a solution.

C) It analyzes a statement made in the first.

D) It makes a contrast.

16. The Voting Rights Act of 1965 helped ensure that states would not be able to enforce regulations that inhibited certain people—mainly African Americans—from voting.

    More African Americans in the South—many of whom had survived living under segregation—were finally able to exercise their right to vote as a result of this Act.

    What does the underlined sentence do?

    A) It states an effect.

    B) It provides an example.

    C) It proposes a solution.

    D) It expands on the first sentence.

17. Learning to play a musical instrument is very popular in many schools, and students are encouraged from a young age to study the piano, violin, flute, or to join the school orchestra.

    Today, musical study is discouraged more than ever in the United States due to budget cuts for the arts, but many argue that it is more important to spend money on supplementary math and science teaching instead.

    What does the underlined sentence do?

    A) It draws a conclusion about what is stated in the first.

    B) It makes a contrast.

    C) It contradicts the first.

    D) It proposes a solution.

18. Beekeeping is a useful skill for anyone interested in serious gardening, for bees are essential in pollination and can help maintain healthy plants and flowers.

    When one community garden added an apiary, the garden produced twice as many fruits and vegetables than it had the year before, and the flowers were larger and brighter.

What does the underlined sentence do?

A) It provides an example.

B) It analyzes a statement in the first sentence.

C) It makes a contrast.

D) It expands on the first sentence.

19. Flash mobs, or groups of people organized on social media who seemingly randomly appear in public to engage in rambunctious behavior, are an amusing, but harmless, social phenomenon.

    While some find it fun to be part of a flash mob, the same cannot be said for those regular people going about their business only to be interrupted by the annoying antics of the flash mob as it descends upon a busy street corner.

    How do the two sentences relate?

    A) They contradict each other.

    B) They present a contrast.

    C) They present a problem and a solution.

    D) They express roughly the same idea.

20. Many people enjoy a cup of strong coffee in the morning, but some prefer tea due to its lower caffeine content; caffeine can cause tension and "jitters."

    Tea contains less coffee than caffeine, which many consumers find preferable, particularly if they suffer from anxiety or high blood pressure.

    How do the two sentences relate?

    A) They establish a contrast.

    B) They present a contradiction.

    C) They reinforce each other.

    D) They present an argument followed by an example.

21. Scuba diving is a popular pastime for tourists at tropical resorts; however, this activity can threaten the fragile ecosystems of the underwater reefs which divers wish to explore.

    Many diving companies now offer educational courses and training to help educate scuba divers learn to safely navigate the beautiful underwater landscapes they wish to visit without disturbing the wildlife.

How do the two sentences relate?

A) They present a problem and a solution.

B) They reinforce each other.

C) They express roughly the same idea.

D) They present a contradiction.

22. Many young college graduates move to major cities like New York, Los Angeles, and Chicago after finishing school in order to pursue careers in business, the arts, social justice, and other professions; these cities offer abundant opportunities in these fields.

    Despite the myriad opportunities in major American cities for recent graduates seeking professional careers, the cost of living in urban centers like New York, Chicago, Los Angeles and elsewhere is exorbitant, and many young people leave these areas after a few years.

    What does the second sentence do?

    A) It proposes a solution.

    B) It states an effect.

    C) It makes a contrast.

    D) It reinforces the first.

23. Alexander Hamilton and James Madison called for the Constitutional Convention to write a constitution as the foundation of a stronger federal government. Madison and other Federalists like John Adams believed in separation of powers, republicanism, and a strong federal government. Despite the separation of powers that would be provided for in the US Constitution, anti-Federalists like Thomas Jefferson called for even more limitations on the power of the federal government.

    In the context of the passage above, which of the following would most likely NOT support a strong federal government?

    A) Alexander Hamilton

    B) James Madison

    C) John Adams

    D) Thomas Jefferson

The next three questions are based on this passage.

In its most basic form, geography is the study of space; more specifically, it studies the physical space of the earth and the ways in which it interacts with, shapes, and is shaped by its habitants. Geographers look at the world from a spatial perspective. This means that at the center of all geographic study is the question, where? For geographers, the where of any interaction, event, or development is a crucial element to understanding it.

This question of where can be asked in a variety of fields of study, so there are many sub-disciplines of geography. These can be organized into four main categories: 1) regional studies, which examine the characteristics of a particular place, 2) topical studies, which look at a single physical or human feature that impacts the whole world, 3) physical studies, which focus on the physical features of Earth, and 4) human studies, which examine the relationship between human activity and the environment.

24. A researcher studying the relationship between farming and river systems would be engaged in which of the following geographical sub-disciplines?

    A) regional studies

    B) topical studies

    C) physical studies

    D) human studies

25. Which of the following is a concise summary of the passage?

    A) The most important questions in geography are where an event or development took place.

    B) Geography, which is the study of the physical space on earth, can be broken down into four sub-disciplines.

    C) Regional studies is the study of a single region or area.

    D) Geography can be broken down into four sub-disciplines: regional studies, topical studies, physical studies, and human studies.

26. Which of the following best describes the mode of the passage?

    A) expository

    B) narrative

    C) persuasive

    D) descriptive

The next three questions are based on this passage.

It's that time again—the annual Friendswood Village Summer Fair is here! Last year we had a record number of visitors, and we're expecting an even bigger turnout this year. The fair will be bringing back all our traditional food and games, including the famous raffle. This year, we'll have a carousel, petting zoo, and climbing wall (for teenagers and adults only, please). We're also excited to welcome Petey's BBQ and Happy Tummy's Frozen Treats, who are both new to the fair this year. Tickets are available online and at local retailers.

27. Which of the following will NOT be a new presence at the Fair this year?

    A) the raffle

    B) the petting zoo

    C) the carousel

    D) Petey's BBQ

28. Based on the context, which of the following is the meaning of the word *record* in the passage?

    A) a piece of evidence

    B) a disk with a groove that reproduces sound

    C) the best or most remarkable

    D) to set down in writing

29. Which of the following best describes the mode of the passage?

    A) expository

    B) narrative

    C) persuasive

    D) descriptive

SENTENCE SKILLS

Directions for questions 1 – 12: In the following questions, select the answer that best rewrites the underlined portion of the sentence. Note that the first answer choice indicates no change was made to the sentence.

1. To horseback ride, surf, and rock climb are Terrence's favorite activities.

   A) To horseback ride, surf, and rock climb
   B) To horseback riding, surfing, and rock climbing
   C) Horseback ride, surf, and rock climb
   D) Horseback riding, surfing, and rock climbing

2. When puffing out the neck, this is a courtship ritual for the anole lizard.

   A) When puffing out the neck, this
   B) Lizards puff out their necks, this
   C) Puffing out the neck
   D) The fact that lizards puff out their necks

3. Writing daily journal entries, which is an activity meant to improve writing skills and creativity.

   A) entries, which is an activity
   B) entries is an activity because it is
   C) entries, being an activity which is
   D) entries is an activity

4. While staying up late to finish homework, an exam, I remembered, I needed to prepare for the next day.

   A) an exam, I remembered, I needed to prepare for
   B) I remembered I needed to prepare for an exam
   C) an exam I remembered I needed to prepare for
   D) there was an exam, I remembered, for it I needed to prepare

5. For a rat, grinding its teeth together quickly, or chattering, is extremely happy.

   A) For a rat, grinding its teeth
   B) A rat grinding its teeth
   C) When a rat grinds its teeth
   D) To grind its teeth, for a rat

6. Trained all her life, Tatyana set a world record for weight lifting.

   A) Trained all her life,
   B) After training all her life,
   C) To train all her life,
   D) As she trained all her life,

7. To seem like they understand our every word, dogs actually only understand the tone and inflection of human language.

   A) To seem like they understand our every word,
   B) To seem like they understand words,
   C) As it seems like they understand our every word
   D) While it seems like they understand our every word,

8. He was intrigued by the House of Romonov searching for a book about the Russian family.

   A) He was intrigued by the House of Romonov searching
   B) He was intrigued by the House of Romonov searched
   C) Intrigued by the House of Romonov, he searched
   D) The House of Romonov intrigued him, searching

9. Embarrassed, he blushed, and his face turned a bright red.

   A) Embarrassed, he blushed, and his face turned a bright red.
   B) He, embarrassed blushed, and his face
   C) His face was embarrassed, and
   D) His face, he blushed, and

10. Controversial as it was, the author stood by her new book.

   A) Controversial as it was, the author stood by her new book.

   B) The author stood by her new book, controversial as it was.

   C) Controversial, the author, as it was, stood by her new book.

   D) The author stood by her, controversial as it was, new book.

11. The information gathered from the census is used to determine political boundaries and planning transportation systems.

   A) to determine political boundaries and planning transportation systems.

   B) determines political boundaries and plans transportation systems.

   C) to determine political boundaries and planning transportation systems.

   D) to determine political boundaries and plan transportation systems.

12. Many artists and producers disagree over how copyright laws should be applied, they have different perspectives on what best protects and encourages creativity.

   A) should be applied, they have different perspectives

   B) should be applied because they have different perspectives

   C) should apply on differing perspectives

   D) are applied with different perspectives

Directions for questions 13-25: Select the answer that begins to rewrite the following sentences most effectively and without changing the meaning of the original sentence. Keep in mind that not every answer choice will complete the original sentence.

13. River otters mate for life, but the same cannot be said of sea otters.

   Rewrite, beginning with:

   Unlike sea otters,—

   The next words will be:

   A) the same cannot be said

   B) river otters mate

   C) they don't mate

   D) river otters don't mate

14. While many states have some form of income tax, Texans only pay federal income tax.

   Rewrite, beginning with:

   Texans only pay federal income tax,—

   The next words will be:

   A) but many other states have

   B) and many states have

   C) and even though many states

   D) therefore many states have

15. Not only can Mimic octopi change colors, they can mimic the shape and texture of many aquatic animals.

   Rewrite, beginning with:

   Mimic octopi can mimic the shape and texture of many aquatic animals—

   The next words will be:

   A) and only change color

   B) but also change color

   C) and change color

   D) only change colors

16. Despite being the founder of Apple, Steve Jobs limited his children's technology usage.

   Rewrite, beginning with:

   Steve Jobs limited his children's technology usage—

   The next words will be:

   A) and he was the

   B) even though he was

   C) as he was

   D) therefore he was

17. The actress was astounded when she won the Oscar.

   Rewrite, beginning with:

   After winning the Oscar,—

   The next words will be:

   A) astonished.

   B) she was astounded.

   C) feeling astounded

   D) the actress was astounded.

18. The gas prices dropped, and people rushed to the pumps.

Rewrite, beginning with:

People rushed to the pumps—

The next words will be:

A) and the gas prices dropped.

B) and then the gas prices dropped.

C) when the gas prices dropped.

D) but the gas prices dropped.

19. After years of paying off loans, Tomas was debt-free.

Rewrite, beginning with:

Tomas was debt-free—

The next words will be:

A) having paid off loans for years.

B) paying off loans for years.

C) and paid off loans for years.

D) despite having paying off loans for years.

20. Wolf packs have intricate social groups, similar to humans.

Rewrite, beginning with:

Like humans,—

The next words will be:

A) wolf packs have

B) wolf packs do not have

C) having an intricate

D) intricate social groups have

21. The train arrived at the station, and passengers began to disembark.

Rewrite, beginning with:

Passengers began to disembark—

The next words will be:

A) and the train arrived

B) before the train arrived

C) after the train arrived

D) even though the train arrived

22. Even though he enjoyed using Facebook and Instagram, Twitter was a different story.

Rewrite, beginning with:

He didn't enjoy using—

The next words will be:

A) Instagram despite enjoying

B) Facebook and Twitter because

C) Twitter because he enjoyed

D) Twitter, despite enjoying

23. If the photographer had the equipment, she would experiment with wildlife photography.

Rewrite, beginning with:

The photographer cannot experiment with wildlife photography—

The next words will be:

A) when having

B) because she

C) although there

D) with enough

24. Yellow-bellied warblers are often spotted in this community, since they are native to the area.

Rewrite, beginning with:

Being native to the area,—

The next words will be:

A) it is common to spot

B) yellow-bellied warblers are often

C) yellow-bellied warblers in this community

D) in this community yellow-bellied warblers are

25. They wrapped sandwiches and bagged chips when they packed for the picnic.

Rewrite, beginning with:

Packing for the picnic,—

The next words will be:

A) wrapping sandwiches

B) sandwiches and chips were

C) when they wrapped

D) they wrapped sandwiches

WRITEPLACER

Write a multiple-paragraph essay of approximately 300 – 600 words based on the prompt below. Plan, write, review and edit your essay during the time provided, and read the prompt carefully before starting your essay.

In recent years, powerful storms around the world have caused extreme destruction. However, rapid growth of population and cities has continued in vulnerable areas, putting millions at risk. Supporters of development in these areas say that they are the engines of the economy and must be accommodated to keep economic growth high. Opponents insist that development must be limited in the interest of public safety, even if that means limiting economic growth, too. We must find a solution that supports the economy and also protects people.

Write an essay of 300 – 600 words taking a position on whether the growth of cities should continue in areas vulnerable to storms and flooding. Support your position using logic and examples.

ESL – LANGUAGE USE

Choose the answer that correctly completes the sentence.

1. The flight _____, so we will have to wait at the airport.

    A) delays

    B) delayed

    C) is delayed

    D) will delay

2. Please _____ your mom today.

    A) calling

    B) calls

    C) called

    D) call

3. _____ the Eiffel Tower when he visited Paris.

    A) They saw

    B) He seen

    C) They seen

    D) He saw

4. Marie Curie received Nobel prizes in Physics and Chemistry for her _____ in those fields.

    A) has researched

    B) research

    C) researching

    D) researched

5. Where _____ you have lunch?

    A) are

    B) have

    C) did

    D) is

6. Sound travels faster in water _____ in air.

    A) than

    B) more

    C) less

    D) at

7. The Great Barrier Reef is the largest living system _____ the world.

    A) for

    B) about

    C) on

    D) in

8. When _____ arrive in the city?

    A) do she

    B) have she

    C) will she

    D) are she

9. _____ take the bus, don't forget to bring your bus pass.

    A) As you

    B) So you

    C) When you

    D) Though you

10. Grace Hopper is famous _____ the first compiler for a programming language.

    A) for having invented

    B) for inventing

    C) her invention

    D) in inventing

11. Because Robert didn't study, he was _____ that his test grade was one of the highest in the class.

    A) disappointed

    B) bored

    C) interested

    D) surprised

12. After the interview, she felt confident that she had impressed the interviewer.

    A) After

    B) During

    C) Later

    D) Before

13. Vero and Joey always help one another with homework, so it is ___ that they will study for the test together this afternoon.

    A) expecting

    B) expected

    C) surprising

    D) surprised

Select the answer that best combines the two sentences.

14. Reese loves playing video games. His sister Melody loves playing video games, too.

    A) Both Reese and his sister Melody love playing video games.

    B) Reese and his sister Melody loves playing video games.

    C) Reese loves playing video games and Melody loves playing video games.

    D) Reese and Melody too love to play video games.

15. Aaliyah thought that it might rain today. She packed her umbrella.

    A) Aaliyah thought that it might rain today, packing her umbrella.

    B) Aaliyah thought that it might rain today, so she packed her umbrella.

    C) Aaliyah thought that it might rain today because she packed her umbrella.

    D) Aaliyah thought that it might rain today when she packed her umbrella.

16. The newest book went on sale. We quickly made our way to the nearest store.

    A) We quickly made our way to the nearest store the newest book went on sale.

    B) When the newest book went on sale, we quickly made our way to the nearest store.

    C) Quickly making our way to the nearest store, the newest book went on sale.

    D) We quickly made our way to the nearest store, so the newest book went on sale.

17. Bamboo can grow nearly three feet in one day. Bamboo is a fast-growing plant.

    A) Being a fast-growing plant, bamboo can grow nearly three feet in one day.

    B) After being a fast-growing plant, bamboo can grow nearly three feet in one day.

    C) Bamboo is a fast-growing plant despite growing nearly three feet in one day.

    D) If bamboo is a fast-growing plant, it grows nearly three feet in one day.

18. The fastest land animal is the cheetah. Cheetahs can reach speeds up to seventy miles an hour.

    A) Cheetahs are the fastest land animal, reached speeds up to seventy miles an hour.

    B) After being the fastest land animal, cheetahs can reach speeds up to seventy miles an hour.

    C) Cheetahs can reach speeds up to seventy miles an hour despite being the fastest land animal.

    D) Reaching speeds up to seventy miles an hour, cheetahs are the fastest land animal.

19. The scientific method helps researchers. It helps them focus their studies and test their hypotheses.

    A) The scientific method helps researchers, and it helps them focus their studies and test their hypotheses.

    B) Researchers use the scientific method, and it helps them focus their studies and test their hypotheses.

    C) The scientific methods helps researchers to focus their studies and test their hypotheses.

    D) Researchers focus their studies and test their hypotheses with the help of the scientific method.

20. Malik loves flying kites. Therefore, his father bought him a new kite for his birthday.

    A) Malik loves flying kites, for his father had bought him a new kite for his birthday.

    B) Malik loves flying kites when his father bought him a new kite for his birthday.

    C) Because Malik loves flying kites, his father bought him a new one for his birthday.

    D) Because his father bought Malik one for his birthday, he loves flying kites.

21. There was a lot of traffic. She called her boss to tell him she would be late for work.

    A) There was a lot of traffic when she called her boss to tell him she would be late for work.

    B) There was a lot of traffic, so she called her boss to tell him she would be late for work.

    C) After she called her boss to tell him she would be late for work, there was a lot of traffic.

    D) She had been calling her boss to tell him she would be late for work before there was a lot of traffic.

22. Emma loved to make chocolate chip cookies. She made them every Sunday for her family.

    A) While Emma loved to make chocolate chip cookies, she had made them every Sunday for her family.

    B) After making them every Sunday for her family, Emma loved to make chocolate chip cookies.

    C) Emma loved to make chocolate chip cookies because she made them every Sunday for her family.

    D) Emma loved to make chocolate chip cookies, so she made them for her family every Sunday.

23. Every night Michelle watches the news. She wants to be informed about current events.

    A) Every night Michelle watches the news, but she wants to be informed about current events.

    B) Michelle stays informed about current events even though she watches the news every night.

C) To watch the news every night, Michelle is informed about current events.

D) Michelle watches the news every night because she wants to be informed about current events.

Read the question and select the best answer.

24. Which of the following is a compound sentence?

    A) Plague, generally not a major public health concern, actually continues to spread among rodent populations today, and it even occasionally makes its way into a human host.

    B) Modern archeology, which seeks answers to humanity's questions about its past, is helped significantly by new technologies.

    C) In the fight against obesity, countries around the world are imposing taxes on sodas and other sugary drinks in an effort to curb unhealthy habits.

    D) Because the assassination of President John F. Kennedy continues to haunt and fascinate Americans, new movies, books, and television series about it are being released every year.

25. Parrots, among the most intelligent birds in the world, have been prized pets for many centuries; in fact, the first recorded instance of parrot training was written in the thirteenth century.

    Which of the following is a synonym for *prized* as used in the sentence?

    A) unlikely

    B) misunderstood

    C) rewarded

    D) valued

26. Her new tennis racket cost her a hundred bucks, but it was worth the steep price tag.

    Which of the following words from the sentence is slang?

    A) cost

    B) bucks

    C) steep

    D) tag

ESL – Reading Skills

1. Chapel Hill, North Carolina, is a popular college town. Home to the University of North Carolina, Chapel Hill is populated by students and other young people, giving this town a lively feel. Chapel Hill is famous for its annual street fair, which especially supports local artists—visual artists, musicians, and performance artists. In fact, the town features murals for the public to enjoy on a daily basis. And of course, everyone supports the popular university sports teams.

   According to the passage, Chapel Hill—

   A) is home to North Carolina's professional sports teams

   B) is where the University of North Carolina is located

   C) is not popular with students and other young people

   D) is where the University of South Carolina is located

2. Good dental care is important, and everyone can take steps to protect their teeth. First, all people should visit their dentist at least once a year for a check-up and thorough cleaning. Dentists can determine if there are any potential problems with teeth or related health issues. Next, everyone should brush their teeth at least twice a day, and replace toothbrushes every three months. Most people should floss once a day or once every other day. Many people benefit from rinsing after brushing and flossing with fluoride rinses or mouthwashes that fight plaque. Finally, everyone benefits from limiting consumption of sugar, which is harmful to teeth. There are many easy ways to promote dental health.

   What is the main idea of this passage?

   A) Brushing your teeth is less important than visiting the dentist.

   B) Brushing your teeth is more important than eating less sugar.

   C) Taking care of your teeth is important and difficult.

   D) Taking care of your teeth is important, but easy to do with a little effort.

3. New York City can be a great place to raise a family. There are lots of parks and playgrounds for children, and plenty of good schools. It is easy for families of any income to get around on foot or using public transportation. Moreover, New York has an abundance of cultural opportunities. With countless museums, galleries, theaters and musical performances year-round, it is one of the most diverse cities in the world.

   What is the main idea of this passage?

   A) New York City is a great place to visit.

   B) There are more opportunities for children in New York City than for adults.

   C) New York City has opportunities for families of different income levels.

   D) New York City has many cultural events.

4. In the U.S., the states of the Great Plains include North and South Dakota, Nebraska, Kansas, and Oklahoma. Parts of eastern Montana, Wyoming, Colorado, and New Mexico also fall within the Great Plains, as does northwestern Texas. Historically the Great Plains were home to millions of buffalo, which were hunted by Native Americans. As the United States grew, the land was conquered and buffalo were killed, making way for white settlers who used the land for cattle ranching and eventually agriculture. Railroads allowed farmers to sell their crops in cities more easily. Today, many people have left the states of the Great Plains to pursue careers and livelihoods where opportunities in business and technology are more abundant in major cities elsewhere in the United States. However, new opportunities have appeared in Plains cities like Omaha and Oklahoma City and in the oil and gas industry in North Dakota.

   Which of the following is implied in the passage above?

A) The states of the Great Plains may start growing again thanks to new opportunities in North Dakota and in cities like Omaha and Oklahoma City.

B) Difficulties in North Dakota and in cities like Omaha and Oklahoma City have caused many people to move away from the Plains states.

C) White settlers used the Great Plains for cattle ranching and agriculture.

D) Native Americans lived off the buffalo found on the Great Plains.

5. A government program to offer working mothers extra money for food and childcare supplies is in danger of being eliminated, due to budget cuts. Some women in the community are writing their local government representative to protest these budget cuts. In fact, one local mother is planning to run for Congress herself.

It is likely that the author believes that:

A) The women in the community do not need extra money for food, just childcare supplies.

B) The local government representative cannot help the community.

C) The woman running for office will change the policy as a member of Congress.

D) The women in the community will not be able to change anything.

6. Many people enjoy collecting coins. This hobby requires a strong knowledge of history and of different cultures. Use of coins goes back thousands of years to ancient times, and civilizations around the world have used them as currency. Some coins are very valuable. However, many collectors enjoy studying and collecting these historical objects regardless of their economic value.

Coin collectors—

A) usually make a lot of money from their hobby

B) have a strong knowledge of history and different cultures

C) possess valuable coins that are worth a lot of money

D) have used coins since ancient times

7. The state of Texas was an independent country before becoming part of the United States. Part of Mexico for centuries, Texas was settled by people of European descent coming from the young United States. These settlers eventually rebelled against Mexico, and Texas declared independence in 1836. A decade of political and military conflict would follow; Texas would later join the United States.

The Texan Revolution was led by

A) people of European descent who had settled in Texas from the United States.

B) people of European descent who had settled in Texas from Mexico.

C) people from Europe and Mexico.

D) people from the United States and Europe.

9. Many high school students have temporary jobs during their summer vacations. Summer businesses like ice cream shops, tourist attractions, and swimming pools provide opportunities for teenagers to earn money and learn responsibility during their time off from school. These jobs also offer teenagers the chance to learn skills like accounting, food handling safety, and lifeguarding; these skills can help them in their studies and as they start to consider career paths.

From this passage, a reader can conclude that the author believes that:

A) Summer jobs are good for teenagers who need extra money, but do not offer life skills.

B) Most teenagers would benefit from having summer jobs.

C) Summer jobs do not offer enough money to teens.

D) Summer businesses should be open year-round.

10. Many members of the community go to the neighborhood health clinic for regular medical treatment. The clinic offers free care to children under the age of five, and free counseling in nutrition for children and pregnant women. Some politicians want to cut funding for the clinic, but community leaders have been able to keep it open through grassroots fundraising in

cooperation with local community groups, churches, and private citizens.

Grassroots fundraising means—

A) getting money from the government

B) getting money from relatives outside of the country

C) getting money from local people and organizations

D) getting money from big companies

11. Many phone companies offer families annual group rates to save money on telephone, internet and text message charges. However, customers often complain about extra fees that cause their phone bills to be higher than they had expected. Citizens have complained to their government representatives about unfair marketing and trade practices by communications companies in this regard. As a result, some phone companies have begun to simplify their billing practices. In addition, smaller phone companies have emerged that offer prepaid or monthly plans with fewer fees and more straightforward charges.

What is the main idea of this passage?

A) Smaller phone companies are a better option for customers who are upset with big phone companies.

B) Big phone companies treat their customers unfairly.

C) Customers are upset because phone companies have unfair billing practices.

D) Government action and more market competition have forced big phone companies to develop more fair billing practices.

12. Chicago is the third-largest city in the United States. Located on the shores of Lake Michigan, Chicago is home to the Willis Tower, the tallest building in the U.S.; the Art Institute of Chicago, with world-renowned exhibitions; and Wrigley Field, home of the popular (if unlucky) Chicago Cubs, one of America's most famous baseball teams. Chicagoans enjoy cuisines from around the world. And, of course, any given night of the week music lovers can find great jazz and blues performers in the many clubs in this center of American music.

This passage implies that:

A) the Willis Tower is the tallest building in the U.S.

B) Chicago is located on a lake.

C) Chicago is an important center for jazz and blues music.

D) Chicago is not a very exciting city.

13. Toussaint L'Ouverture was the leader of the Haitian Revolution, when slaves in Haiti rebelled against France, eventually winning their freedom and the independence of Haiti. L'Ouverture was a talented political and military leader, and he formed international alliances to support Haitian independence and freedom for the slaves. Although he died before independence was formally declared, his legacy continues as a fighter for justice and freedom.

It is likely that the author believes that:

A) Haiti and France had a good relationship before Haitian independence.

B) Haiti did not have international support in its struggle for freedom.

C) Toussaint L'Ouverture will not be remembered by many.

D) Toussaint L'Ouverture was a great leader worthy of respect.

14. Niagara Falls is a popular destination for tourists. In the summer, tourists can take boats around the spectacular waterfall, and they can spend time exploring the local regions of upstate New York and southern Ontario. The city of Toronto is not far away. During the winter, sometimes the falls freeze over into enormous frozen icicles, amazing visitors. The falls rest right on the border between the United States and Canada, so tourists must remember to bring their passports if they wish to take advantage of all the attractions the region has to offer.

Visitors to Niagara Falls should bring a passport because:

A) Niagara Falls is located on an international border, so interesting attractions may be located in another country.

B) Visitors require a passport if they wish to explore the falls by boat.

C) All visitors need a passport if they would like to travel to Toronto.

D) Niagara Falls is located on an international border, so it is impossible to visit the waterfall without a passport.

15. Roy and Leticia each work two jobs. Roy works for the water company as a technician and drives a taxi at night. Leticia is a medical assistant and takes care of her neighbor's children four nights a week, in addition to watching her own two sons. Once a week, Leticia goes to a medical class at the community college to improve her career opportunities. Both Roy and Leticia go to church on Sundays and participate in church activities on Sunday afternoons with their families.

From this passage, which of these statements can the reader assume?

A) Roy is planning to go to school part-time.

B) Both Roy and Leticia are extremely busy and would probably enjoy a vacation.

C) Roy is worried that he will lose his job with the water company.

D) Leticia does not enjoy spending time with her neighbor's children.

16. The Museum of Natural Science has opened an exhibit about the ecology of the Columbia River Basin. The exhibit includes plants, insects, birds, and mammals that are unique to the Columbia River Basin and explores the changes that have occurred in this delicate ecosystem over the last century. The exhibit has exciting audio-visual presentations. Individual tickets are available on the museum's website, and groups may apply for special ticket prices by calling the museum directly.

According to the passage, individuals can purchase tickets to the exhibit—

A) at the museum

B) for a special price

C) by phone

D) online

17. Nocturnal animals are animals that sleep during the day and are active at night. They may search for food, hunt, breed, fight, play, or do any other activity throughout the night, returning to their nests or lairs at sunrise to rest until sundown, when they come out again. Nocturnal animals are found throughout the United States and Canada and include bats, owls, certain species of cats, foxes, raccoons, possums, and more.

What is the main idea of the passage?

A) Nocturnal animals sleep during the day.

B) Many animals around the world are nocturnal.

C) Nocturnal animals are active at night and common throughout North America.

D) Nocturnal animals, animals that are active at night, are unusual in North America.

ESL – Sentence Meaning

Complete the sentence with the correct word or phrase.

1. The children helped to _____ the laundry.

   A) hang around

   B) hang out

   C) hang on

   D) hang up

2. After she went to the store, Denise _____ to pick up the laundry.

   A) need to

   B) had to

   C) have to

   D) will have to

3. Even though he is the _____ kitten of the group, Noodle is the most playful.

   A) smallest

   B) smaller

   C) more smallest

   D) most small

4. My friend asked me to help her _____ to her new apartment.

   A) move out

   B) move through

   C) move in

   D) move to

5. I forgot to _____ what you said— would you mind repeating it?

   A) write over

   B) write back

   C) write on

   D) write down

6. She needed new shoes; the shoes she was wearing were _____.

   A) worn up

   B) worn out

   C) worn over

   D) worn off

7. Until the 1980s, when teachers arrived from out of state, the best teachers at the school _____ at the university in Seattle.

   A) were studied

   B) have studied

   C) had studied

   D) will have studied

8. Sheila and Maria hate broccoli; they think it tastes _____ out of all the vegetables.

   A) the worst

   B) worst

   C) the worse

   D) worse

Read the sentence(s), then answer the question.

9. Mia feels under the weather, so she is staying home today.

   Mia feels—

   A) cold

   B) sick

   C) hot

   D) worried

10. Don't waste time when grading papers for Professor Huang, because she means business.

    Professor Huang—

    A) is serious about her work

    B) is angry about business

    C) is easily angered

    D) wishes to focus on business instead of schoolwork

11. Josh always cracks me up.

    Josh—

    A) makes people angry

    B) makes people uncomfortable

    C) is friendly

    D) is very funny

12. Christopher doesn't like visiting family, going on trips, or meeting new people.

Christopher is most likely—

A) lonely

B) boring

C) unfriendly

D) unhappy

13. France is known for its excellent cuisine; tourists often visit restaurants when in the country.

According to the sentence, what is France famous for?

A) tourism

B) food

C) museums

D) art

14. Danny works on and off for his father.

How often does Danny work for his father?

A) regularly

B) on weekends

C) sometimes

D) never

15. Rachel and Jacqueline booked a flight for next Tuesday.

Rachel and Jacqueline—

A) got airplane tickets for Tuesday's flight

B) will buy airplane tickets next Tuesday

C) purchased a book of tickets on Tuesday

D) bought airplane tickets on Tuesday

16. Sara got used to the air conditioning in her office.

Sara—

A) was uncomfortable with the air conditioning

B) did not use the air conditioning

C) began to use the air conditioning

D) became accustomed to the air conditioning

17. Samuel was able to lift more weights than any other man at the gym.

Of all the men at the gym, Sam was the—

A) stronger

B) more strong

C) strongest

D) most stronger

18. Diana meant to call her brother yesterday, but she got busy taking care of the children.

Diana—

A) intended to call her brother

B) did not want to call her brother

C) tried to call her brother

D) was not allowed to call her brother

19. Of all the summers on record, this one has been the hottest.

How does this summer compare to other summers in history?

A) It is less hot.

B) It is about the same.

C) It is the most hot.

D) It is hotter than some, but not others.

20. I promised my mother that I would keep an eye on my little brother.

I promised my mother that I would—

A) look for my little brother

B) watch my little brother

C) find my little brother

D) play with my little brother

21. It is not easy to run a business; you must be organized and hardworking.

It is important to be organized and hardworking—

A) in order to manage a business

B) to easily run from business

C) not to ruin a business

D) in order to do business

ANSWER KEY

Arithmetic

1.	B)	6.	A)	11.	D)	16.	B)
2.	C)	7.	D)	12.	B)	17.	A)
3.	C)	8.	D)	13.	B)	18.	D)
4.	D)	9.	C)	14.	D)		
5.	A)	10.	C)	15.	D)		

Elementary Algebra

1.	D)	6.	C)	11.	C)	16.	C)
2.	D)	7.	A)	12.	A)	17.	D)
3.	C)	8.	C)	13.	C)	18.	B)
4.	A)	9.	B)	14.	C)	19.	B)
5.	A)	10.	C)	15.	D)	20.	C)

College-Level Math

1.	D)	6.	D)	11.	D)	16.	A)
2.	B)	7.	B)	12.	A)	17.	C)
3.	E)	8.	A)	13.	D)	18.	C)
4.	C)	9.	B)	14.	C)	19.	E)
5.	A)	10.	C)	15.	B)	20.	B)

Reading Comprehension

1.	B)	9.	C)	17.	C)	25.	B)
2.	C)	10.	C)	18.	A)	26.	A)
3.	A)	11.	B)	19.	A)	27.	A)
4.	C)	12.	B)	20.	C)	28.	C)
5.	D)	13.	B)	21.	A)	29.	C)
6.	D)	14.	B)	22.	C)		
7.	A)	15.	D)	23.	D)		
8.	D)	16.	A)	24.	D)		

Sentence Skills

1.	D)	8.	C)	15.	C)	22.	D)
2.	C)	9.	A)	16.	B)	23.	B)
3.	D)	10.	B)	17.	D)	24.	B)
4.	B)	11.	D)	18.	C)	25.	D)
5.	B)	12.	B)	19.	A)		
6.	B)	13.	B)	20.	A)		
7.	D)	14.	A)	21.	C)		

ESL – Language Use

1.	C)	8.	C)	15.	B)	22.	D)
2.	D)	9.	C)	16.	B)	23.	D)
3.	D)	10.	B)	17.	A)	24.	A)
4.	B)	11.	D)	18.	D)	25.	D)
5.	C)	12.	A)	19.	C)	26.	B)
6.	A)	13.	B)	20.	C)		
7.	D)	14.	A)	21.	B)		

ESL – Reading Skills

1.	B)	6.	B)	11.	D)	16.	D)
2.	D)	7.	A)	12.	C)	17.	C)
3.	C)	8.	C)	13.	D)		
4.	A)	9.	B)	14.	A)		
5.	C)	10.	C)	15.	B)		

ESL – Sentence Meaning

1.	D)	7.	C)	13.	B)	19.	C)
2.	B)	8.	A)	14.	C)	20.	B)
3.	A)	9.	B)	15.	A)	21.	A)
4.	C)	10.	A)	16.	D)		
5.	D)	11.	D)	17.	C)		
6.	B)	12.	C)	18.	A)		

CPSIA information can be obtained
at www.ICGtesting.com
Printed in the USA
LVOW09s1504271016
510551LV00007B/404/P

9 781941 743874